SOUTHWOOD NAZARENE
CHRISTIAN SCHOOL

W9-CVS-223

To Those Who Teach in Christian Schools

Roy W. Lowrie, Jr., Ed. D.

Headmaster
Delaware County Christian School
Newtown Square, Pa.
(K-12)

Foreword by Gene Garrick

published by

Association of Christian Schools International
P.O. Box 4097, Whittier, California 90607

Second Printing

All Rights Reserved

No portion of this book may be reproduced in any way without the written permission of the publisher, except for brief excerpts in magazine reviews, etc.

To Those Who Teach
in Christian Schools

© Copyrighted 1978, Roy W. Lowrie, Jr.
Printed in The United States of America

CONTENTS

Committees — Lesson Planning — Pre-School Orientation — Faculty Meetings — Time — Reporting to Parents — Bulletin Board and Furnishings — Record Keeping — Standardized Tests — Students with Physical Needs — Accidents and Injuries — Playground, Bus, and Cafeteria Duty — Visitors — Student Teachers — New Faculty and Staff Members — Student Career Guidance — Professionalism

Supporting Activities — Sponsoring Activities — The P.T.F. — Faculty Socials — District or Regional Christian School Meetings — Perspective on Activities — Activity Groups and the Community — School Publications and Press Releases — Lending a Helping Hand — Home, and Home Visits — Serious Illness or Accidents — Handling Student Money — Long Range Activity Planning — Student Fund Raising Activities — Encouraging Students in Activities — Encouraging Parent Support of Activities — Behaviour at Athletic Events — Chaperoning Activities — Social Needs of Students — Encouraging Church Activities

Understanding the Organizational Structure — Following the Chain of Command — Respect for the School Board — The Faculty Handbook — Enforcing School Policies — Faculty Dress Code — Criticism — Discussing Students with other Parents — Answering Common Questions — Direct Dealing with the Principal — The Contract — Leaving the School — Scheduling Field Trips and Activities — Ordering Books, Supplies, Etc.

Commitment to Excellence — Handling Pressures — Courage with Parents — Accept Reproof — Punctuality — Requesting Help — No Racial Prejudice — Sound Judgment — Talking Too Much — Housekeeping Responsibilities — Care of Equipment and Furniture — Circumstantial Leading — Flexibility — Attitude Toward Staff Members — A Procrustean Attitude — Continued Interest in Former Students —

Loyalty — Honesty — Daily Attendance — Home
Conditions — Appearance and Grooming — Being
Approachable — Sense of Humor — Personal Finance
— Family Priority — Moonlighting — Patience —
Close of the Year

To the faculty and staff
of the
Delaware County Christian School
Newtown Square, Pennsylvania
my professional colleagues,
my friends, and my co-workers
in the Lord.

Betty J. Barteit, L. Suzanne Sink, Beth E. Allen, Terry W. Sullivan, Linda A. Sherman, Margaret S. Lowrie, Janice Chase, Marcey S. Shockley, Norma J. La Shure, Susan K. Hutchison, Mary Ellen Bough, Ellen J. Anderson, Nancy J. Walker, Leone M. Lauffer, Jean G. Linder, Eleanor M. Hayes, Rose M. Warkentin, Mary A. Piepgrass, Robert S. Signorino, Paul G. Sweeny, Carmen L. Fuentes, Dwight L. Fowler, Marilyn R. Ykema, Stephen P. Dill, Renee J.W. Wewer, Lucille Johnston, Dawn K. Stirneman, Nancy R. Jacobson, Douglas C. Haring, William J. Calderwood, Suzanne K. Calderwood, George K. McFarland, P. Ivan Akers, Freda Baker, William H. Tobin, Jr., Crystal E. Schwartz, George A. Husmann, Maynard L. Gray, Christopher D. Maffett, Larry M. Lake, Gwen E. Prestwood, Louella M. True, Leona F. Eyler, Dorothy E. Merola, Isla M. Hopson, Patricia E. Sweely, Frank H. Roberts, Alex Szucs, Joe R. Hoekstra, John R. Lasco, Janet M. Ash, Ardith DeLong.

"Therefore, my beloved brethren, be ye steadfast, unmoveable, always abounding in the work of the Lord, forasmuch as ye know that your labour is not in vain in the Lord."

I Corinthians 15:58

FOREWORD

There is a difference between a Christian teacher and a teacher who is a Christian. Too often a teacher who is a Christian moves into the Christian school classroom and carries the same secular bent toward the subjects and even the students which was present in the non-Christian school. In contrast, the truly Christian teacher assures that all the teaching, activities and relationships are in alignment with his Christian view of life and with the teaching of Scripture. In 1954, Dr. Frank Gaebelein wrote in his definitive work, THE PATTERN OF GOD'S TRUTH, concerning the problem of giving a truly God-centered education in our Christian schools: "Yes, the crux of the problem lies with the teacher. The fact is inescapable; the world view of the teacher, insofar as he is effective, gradually conditions the world view of the pupil. No man teaches out of a philosophical vacuum. In one way or another, every teacher expresses the convictions he lives by, whether they be spiritually positive or negative. This is why the school . . . that would develop a Christ centered and Biblically grounded program must fly from its masthead this standard, 'No Christian education without Christian teachers, . . .'"

The training of a truly Christian teacher is not done solely in college. In radical contrast to secular education the Christian philosophy of education recognizes the impact of personality on students and must require that the teacher be trained not only in teaching skills but also in godliness; not only in subject areas but in Bible. The influence is not just in the classroom but in the total life of the teacher — attitudes, habits, character, associations, interests, priorities, motivations, reactions and relationships. This means that the training must include professional and personal study of the Scriptures, the discipline and fellowship of the church, a Christian lifestyle and sensitivity to the Holy Spirit.

Where do teachers get this training? Some have received it

from childhood in a godly home. Others have been discipled by a Christian brother or sister, or by a local church involvement, or through a Christian school or college. Many do not have such training. No one is trained so thoroughly in Christian living and thinking that no further help is needed. The Christian school itself must also carry out a continuing program of education for its teachers, especially in the philosophy of Christian school education and its application to the curriculum. Most schools do something, but often even this is inadequate due to the press of other duties. A book such as this one will, therefore, meet an urgent need in the Christian school movement.

Dr. Lowrie brings a quarter of a century of experience to bear on the unique training needed for the teacher in a Christian school. He has worked with scores of teachers as headmaster and hundreds more as a consultant, workshop leader and spokesman for the Christian school movement, which he has in a large measure helped to shape. The practical advice and instructions given are based on a high degree of success in giving quality Christian education to children, their parents and the author's own staff.

The chapters are written to give immediate help where most needed. By use of the detailed listing of contents a teacher can find answers to particular problems and questions about Christian school practices and how the teacher approaches them. Yet, mixed in with these down-to-earth observations and underlying all of them is a clear, simple statement of Christian school philosophy. Since all practice is based on philosophy, this is vital. Every Christian school teacher and administrator needs in-depth reading in philosophy, and I recommend it; but a careful inquiry into and meditation on the underlying presuppositions of this book will yield rich insights.

Administrators will find help in teacher orientation and in-service education. The book could be given to the whole staff and studied throughout the year — bit by bit in faculty meetings or in a staff retreat. It is a must for teachers new to the school and can be very helpful for that teacher who wants to understand how teaching in a Christian school differs from teaching in other schools. Board members should read it to understand the qualities to look for in hiring the faculty. Future teachers should study it in college.

The Christian school movement is one raised up of God. TO THOSE WHO TEACH IN CHRISTIAN SCHOOLS, along with others Dr. Lowrie has written for administrators and board members, will give it direction, depth and quality.

Gene Garrick
Pastor
The Tabernacle Church
Norfolk, VA

Preface

Each school year I have frequent opportunities to give visitors a tour of our school's buildings and grounds. This is a blessing to me because of the chance to recount God's faithfulness over a period of years in supplying excellent facilities for elementary school children and for high school young people through the sacrifice and offerings of many of His people. The Delaware County Christian School is a testimony to the faithfulness of God to His people who claimed Jeremiah 32:17.

Upon the completion of the tour most visitors make some comments about the classrooms, the science facilities, the libraries, or the gymnasiums. At that point I quietly explain that we thank God for facilities and equipment, but the teachers are really the heart of the school. Buildings provide the space within which Christian education can take place. The teachers lead the students into an education in which the Lord Jesus Christ is preeminent. They are the gold in the bank.

My wife, Peg, and I thank God for the influence of Christian school teachers on our five children. It is not an exaggeration to say that their impact upon our Janet, Winnie, Ellen, Roy, and Beth has been eternal. Other parents throughout America join us in thanking God for faithful teachers who are teaching in "God's School System."

It is the purpose of this book to share some practical matters with Christian school teachers and with prospective Christian school teachers. It is not written from an adversary position, for Christian school teachers and administrators work in harmony. The book does not arise out of any particular problems. No axe is being ground. It is simply a straightforward discussion of practical matters that should be talked about openly as friends. Understanding what the principal expects of a teacher should strengthen the relationship between the two, both spiritually and professionally.

Although I write as an administrator, I have always taught at least one course and think of myself as a teacher. The thoughts which follow are for me as well as for you. I am not

1

talking at you, but with you. My respect, and my prayers, are with you as you minister each day to the children, young people, and parents whom God has brought to you for this school year.

In closing this preface, I share with you a truth that God is impressing upon me these days. This truth, expressed several places in the Scripture, is this: Be not weary in well doing, for in due season we shall reap if we faint not.

Teaching school is not a glamorous career, but it is pleasing to God. And, that is the purpose of life. Have a good day.

Roy W. Lowrie, Jr., Headmaster
Delaware County Christian School
Malin Road
Newtown Square, PA 19073

Chapter One

IMPORTANT
SPIRITUAL MATTERS

It is a privilege and an honor to teach in a school that has the name Christian in its title. Immediately we are recognized as different, as being on the Lord's side in education. We minister to the spirit of a student as well as to his soul and body. We encourage students to become mighty in the spirit as well as competent in academics.

As Christians we see the spiritual dimension of education which the unregenerate teacher cannot see. They teach knowledge alone, but we teach wisdom and understanding in addition to knowledge. We count spiritual matters to be of prime importance.

To think spiritually, and to communicate spiritually to our students, is not a simplistic matter. To express it another way, Christian school teaching is not the action of that moment, it is the outpouring of the teacher's life. A number of important matters about spiritual teaching are presented in the discussion which follows.

Assurance of Salvation

To represent Christ in the classroom, the teacher must have full assurance that he is a child of God through faith in Christ. A teacher who lacks this assurance disqualifies himself at once from the Christian school profession. Unregenerate teachers cannot teach from the Christian perspective on education and cannot lead students to saving faith in Christ. The school must hire only teachers who know that they are saved.

A Clear Testimony

A teacher who gropes for words in telling how he received Christ is not going to be able to explain the gospel clearly enough for a child or a young person to understand. It is imperative that teachers be soul winners, unusually adept at presenting the gospel clearly and simply so that a lost student can comprehend it.

A teacher whose testimony is a mixture of the gospel plus visions or dreams may know Christ, but may not be clear in his testimony because of the unusual experiences that he has had. The recounting of such experiences can be puzzling to children and if hired, the teacher should be asked to simply share the gospel without the other experiences.

Strong Sense of God's Leading into Teaching

Teaching in the Christian school is not just a job, it is a ministry. This was illustrated recently when a group of ministers and their wives were touring our school. When we entered one of the science laboratories, one of the pastors saw the teacher, who happened to be a member of his church. The pastor said to the teacher, "It's nice to see you in your sanctuary." That teacher has been called of God to serve in the Christian school as definitely as that pastor has been called to his ministry.

Strong Sense of God's Leading To This School

It is important to know that teaching in this particular

Christian school is God's placement for you. That deep conviction helps a teacher to settle in, unpack his bags mentally, and set his hand to the work to be done. An unsettled teacher does not make the strong contribution to the life of the school that is essential to its progress, for he is always thinking or wishing that he were someplace else. Dr. Paul Culley, former dean of the Graduate School of Columbia Bible College, emphasized this years ago when he said that the strongest schools were built where people were giving their lives to it, dying there a day at a time. That commitment comes from the deep conviction that this is the school where God wants you to serve Him.

Close Walk With God

Christian school students do not need a teacher who has a form of godliness, denying the power thereof. They need a teacher who is having fresh experiences with God, who reads the Bible as if it were a newly published book. The teacher's personal walk with God gives vitality to his Bible teaching and credibility to what he shares about God both in and out of the classroom. Students do not benefit from a teacher who is feeding himself on stale manna. Past faith and past experiences should encourage us today to say as Caleb, "Lord, give me this mountain."

Consistent Quiet Time

Personal devotion to God is essential. The day that is started with God's Word and prayer is always more effective than the day when this spiritual exercise is omitted. We need, as Jeremiah, to feed on the Word of God and we will find, as he, that it is sweeter than the honeycomb and is the joy and rejoicing of life.

One of the greatest things a teacher can do for a student is to encourage and direct him into a life of consistent daily devotion to God. Teachers who do not do this themselves will never help students do it.

Primary Concern

The teacher's first concern is his own personal holiness before the Lord. To maintain a continuous, living fellowship with Almighty God through our Lord Jesus Christ is his primary responsibility and is the pre-requisite to representing the Lord Jesus before children in the classroom, in fellowship with other teachers in the day-by-day routine of the school, and in co-operation with the parents and the Board of Trustees. This requires a confidence that God will do all He has promised to do in His Word.

Christian Fellowship

The members of the faculty form an intimate fellowship closely resembling a family. In this interdependency there are various functions and responsibilities that are accepted as God-given. God provides teachers with varied background, training and experience in order that they may complement one another. No one is perfect, nor can anyone be a prima donna. What may be a weakness in one is supplemented by a strength in another; and teachers must be watchful for opportunities in love to foster the unity and completeness of the family. Always there is the necessity for teachers to have the blood of Jesus Christ cleansing us from all sin even while we are walking in fellowship with one another.

Outside Interests

A teacher in the Christian school is expected to make this service to the Lord as central in his interest, his praying, his planning of his life as if he were a missionary teaching children on the foreign field. It is this sort of teacher who is teaching not first of all for the joy of teaching, nor for the sake of earning a living, not even for a love of children, but because the love of Christ constrains him to teach. The teacher's time, his energies, his thoughts, his desires and his anticipations should be concentrated in this work. He must always conduct himself in such a way as to commend his Lord and the work he is doing.

Sensitivity to the Spiritual Needs of Students

Students have individual academic needs and they have individual spiritual needs. A strong teacher is sensitive to the needs in both areas. This does not imply a nosey prying into the student's private life. It is an awareness from the classroom and from activities of the student's needs.

Dr. Anthony C. Fortosis, long time former headmaster of the Ben Lippen School in Asheville, NC, refers to this sensitivity to the spiritual needs of students as a "shepherd's heart". That is well put. We should ask God to develop that heart in us.

Prayer

Writing shortly after the Civil War, E.M. Bounds said that the absence of prayer is a sure sign of work done in the flesh. His words have meaning for us teachers today. James says that the prayers of a righteous man have a powerful effect. Part of the ministry of the teacher is to serve God in daily prayer for our students, parents, colleagues, board, and the alumni.

Miss Lucille Johnston, a widely respected teacher and elementary school principal of the Delaware County Christian School, prayed for every child in her class each day. She kept the roster by her bed and held each child before God daily. She is an effective teacher spiritually as well as academically. God answers her daily prayers as He promises.

A teacher should also participate in the group prayer times during faculty devotions. Care must be taken not to take too large a share of the time. But, care must be taken to be involved. Faculty devotions are not a time to share silence. It is the time to pray.

Soul Winning

The teacher must be able to discern the gracious working of the Holy Spirit in bringing a child under conviction for his sins. Then the teacher must explain the plan of salvation and help the child pray to receive Christ as his Saviour.

A study of western Christian schools by Dr. Paul A. Kienel, Executive Director of the Association of Christian Schools International, revealed that Christian school teachers lead more children to Christ than did Sunday School teachers. If there is one area where teachers should excel it should be soul winning. God says that the person who wins souls is wise.

Understanding the Value of the Student

The Christian school teacher understands that the student is not a higher form of animal life. He is a person, made by God in His image. When regenerated, the student is a child of God.

The natural abilities of the student by reason of his physical birth are in reality God-given. The spiritual gifts of the student by reason of his new birth are God-given by the Spirit as He wills. Saved students, then, are doubly gifted and are to be taught as such.

If anyone should love and respect the student, in addition to his parents, it should be the Christian School teacher.

Meeting Biblical Standards for Spiritual Leadership

The Bible does not mention Christian school teachers, but it does lay down qualifications for leadership in the church. These qualifications are applicable for people in any Christian organization which purposes to do things from the biblical position.

The list for men is from I Timothy 3. The list assumes that the man has been born again. The requirements are: the husband of one wife, vigilant, sober, of good behaviour, given to hospitality, apt to teach, not given to wine, no striker, not greedy of filthy lucre, patient, not a brawler, not covetous, rules his own house well, has his children in subjection, not a novice, grave, not double-tongued; and his wife, grave, faithful, not a slanderer.

The Bible does not give a list similar to I Timothy 3 for women. That passage does say some things, however, and from Proverbs 31 and Titus 2 it seems reasonable to conclude that the following should be considered requirements: born again, behaviour becoming holiness, not false accusers, not given to much wine, teachers of good things, love their husbands and children, chaste, keepers at home, good, and obedient to their own husbands.

It is always possible that a teacher who is qualified at the time of his appointment to the faculty will have a change which makes him unqualified. When that sad event occurs, the honorable thing is for the teacher to resign. If the teacher does not resign, the board must take the difficult action to remove the teacher from the faculty. That is a sobering thought to us teachers. We need to protect our spiritual qualifications for our ministry with all diligence. To illustrate this point, a seminary professor, much respected for 25 years of teaching service, had to resign because of his marriage situation.

Spiritual Head of the Home

The Bible is explicit in saying that the husband is the head of the home. It is important for the teacher to understand his priorities and always to keep them in order. They are, in proper order: 1. God, 2. Family, 3. School. Any rearrangement of this order will cause difficulty over a period of time. Also, if the father fails to be the leader of the home, difficulties are bound to arise. A teacher cannot disregard his home responsibilities and be effective in the school. It does not work like that.

Own Children Properly Disciplined

A teacher whose own children are not well disciplined has disqualified himself. If he cannot control his own children, he cannot be expected to discipline the children of others.

The biblical figure, Eli, is a warning to us. Eli knew how to tell Samuel that it was God calling his name, but Eli did not correct his own sons. In contrast, God said this about Abraham in Genesis 18, "For I know him, that he will command his children and his household after him, and they shall keep the way of the Lord, to do justice and judgment . . ."

Good Reputation as a Parent

The Christian school teacher must be doing right in his own family to be spiritually qualified to teach others. Teachers live in a goldfish bowl under daily scrutiny by everyone. Sometimes this is irritating, but it must be accepted as one of our occupational hazards.

James refers to this in Chapter 3 of his epistle. After saying that not everyone should be a teacher, he asserts that teachers are judged more strictly and carefully. This should not become burdensome; it is just inherent in teaching.

Since the best teaching is by example, the teacher who is godly, whose family relationships are right, whose children are ordered, is teaching great Christian lessons through his family.

High Threshold of Tolerance

Christian school teachers always live with some dissent, with some level of discontent. There is never a time when 100% of the students and parents are completely satisfied. There is always some criticism coming your way from someone.

When teachers are conscientious and are striving to do their best for God, unwarranted criticism hurts. The answer is to trust God each day and endure the hardness accompanying this. Teachers cannot be easily offended, but must tolerate much.

To serve God in the Christian school a teacher must take a great deal. People think that teachers dish out a lot. The reverse is the truth, for we must actually take a great deal. This must be accepted graciously, without rancor or bitterness. A spirit of bitterness quickly overflows thereby defiling many. I Peter 2:21-23 shows Christ as our example in this matter.

Testimony Outside the School

A teacher must have a clear testimony for Christ, off campus as well as on campus. The Bible speaks of Christians being well-spoken of by those who are without, that is, by unbelievers. A teacher invalidates his teaching if he lives like an unregenerate person when he is out of the classroom, out of sight of the school. Such a teacher is a hypocrite, and his teaching will never be effective in the lives of his students.

The Faculty and Staff
as a Spiritual Body

It is good to think of the faculty and staff as a microcosm of the body of Christ. He is the head of the school, and by His Holy Spirit He has led to the school the faculty and staff members whom He wants to serve Him there. The body is to function as one unit under His direction, with an understanding of individual differences, but with great care and love for one another. Scriptural body-life principles must be practiced by all teachers, being careful not to think of staff members as less important parts of the body.

When a Christian school faculty and staff function harmoniously as a body, there is deep blessing from God and a strong sense of personal fulfillment in each person's heart. It is a beautiful, precious thing to experience. By contrast, when body-life principles are not practiced the entire body suffers and the Holy Spirit is grieved. At such times teaching in the Christian school is not a blessing, or even fun. A school cannot go contrary to Scriptural teaching on the body as taught in I Corinthians 12 and experience the blessing of God upon the faculty and staff.

Part of Satan's greatest strategy against Christian schools is in this very area. Some schools are hurt, some of them deeply, because the faculty and staff do not think of themselves as a body and do not keep practicing the principles by which a spiritual body of believers is kept healthy. This is a sad thing to see in a Christian school. It is sadder to experience.

Participation in Faculty Devotions

It is important to be on time to morning devotions, or even a few minutes early for fellowship with others. The teacher who comes in late breaks the spirit of the meeting and seldom participates himself — a dual problem. In foul weather a teacher needs to leave home earlier than usual to be on time to devotions. It is that simple; there is nothing tricky about it.

If the devotions are open for discussion, it is important for each teacher to comment, for in this way we minister to each other and grow ourselves by framing and expressing spiritual thoughts. How many times over the years God has ministered to my spiritual needs through the comments of my colleagues in morning devotions. I am grateful that they spoke out.

The prayer time should emphasize school matters, not our outside spiritual concerns. This does not mean that personal requests are to be squelched. It is simply that prayer should focus upon the school. Prayer requests should be made freely, but with discretion. Sometimes there is wisdom in making an unspoken request. Since the Bible says that men ought always to pray, it is not a matter of "Should I pray?", but "What should I pray about?"

No teacher should dominate devotions by using more than a fair share of time commenting on the Scripture or in praying. The greater danger is in not participating. Morning devotions are not for the purpose of coming together to share silence.

The Authority of the Bible

A Christian school teacher must believe, with no mental reservation, that the Bible is the Word of God. It is essential to hold to the inerrancy, the infallibility, and the authority of the Bible. Any lesser view cannot be tolerated in the school.

The Bible is the key to the Christian philosophy of life and education. If it is not accepted as God's Word, the teacher has lost the key and has nothing truthful to offer the students. To be strong, the school must not hire or must dismiss any teacher not holding this view of the Bible.

Knowledge of the Bible

Dr. Kenneth O. Gangel, President of Miami Christian College, says that a Christian school teacher can be likened to a coin. On one side is the teacher's academic training. On the other side is his biblical training. Each side must be clearly etched for the teacher to be a strong Christian teacher.

The teacher must have a zeal that is in accordance with a knowledge of the Bible. The teacher must rightly divide the Word of Truth, for many wrong ideas come forth when the Scriptures are wrested.

Teachers must use the tools of personal Bible study enough to be quite at ease in going to the Word to find out what God says about a matter. This Bible study will be our life long pursuit and our great joy. Teachers study many books, but none brings the satisfaction of THE BOOK. It affects our hearts, not just our minds. It reaches our spirit.

Understanding of Bible Doctrine

The Christian school teacher must be spiritually discerning to identify false doctrines. False doctrine is growing more prevalent and is widely propagated by false teachers. The Bible says to be established in the Word, not blown about by every wind of doctrine. Warnings are given that false teaching will increase, not decrease, as time goes on.

Teachers need to emphasize the content of the Scriptures. The big question in evaluating various doctrines is, "What saith the Scriptures?" Only the Bible is God's revelation. Its teachings are the truth. Students need to be convinced of this and well grounded in the doctrines of the Bible. We are exhorted to pay attention to doctrine.

Integrating the Bible
With Academic Instruction

Some people think that the Christian school teaches a course in Bible, with the remainder of the day being identical to the secular school. This is not true. It is the genius of the Christian school to bring the biblical viewpoint to bear on every subject and on every activity. Teachers must seek to view all of the educational programs of the school through the Christian window — the Christian lens — which is the Bible. This requires careful and extended thought by the teacher, for most of us were taught in college that there is a dichotomy between secular subjects and sacred subjects. This is taught in most Christian colleges as well as secular universities.

It takes about three years for a new teacher to be reeducated to teach from a true Christian viewpoint. This is why strong schools do not hire short-term teachers. Sometimes this is a difficult process to reason through, for teachers tend to teach as they were taught, and it is not a simple thing to change.

The classic book to study in this regard is *The Pattern of God's Truth*, by Dr. Frank E. Gaebelein, headmaster emeritus of the Stony Book School. The newest book on the topic, and it is an excellent book, is edited by Dr. Paul Kienel, Executive Director of the International Association of Christian Schools. It is entitled, *The Philosophy of Christian School Education*.

Dr. Ruth Haycock, professor of Christian Education at Baptist Bible College of Clarks Summit, Pa., is one of the leading teachers in the area of integrating the Bible with the total educational program of the school. In one of her presentations at the National Institute of Christian School Administration, held each year at Grace College, Winona Lake, Indiana, she commented that the Christian school teacher must make a life-long commitment to seek ways in which to integrate the Bible with the daily work and activities of the students. You cannot read a few books, listen to several tapes, and know it all.

Agreement with the School's Doctrinal Statement

Each Christian school has its own statement of faith. A teacher accepting a contract to minister at that school is obviously asserting that he agrees to that statement with no mental reservation. It would be absolutely wrong to go into a school with the idea of proselyting the students to another doctrinal standard.

Most schools require teachers to sign a statement each year as part of their new contract agreeing that they currently hold to the school's doctrinal statement. This protects the school from the teacher who comes believing the doctrinal statement, but who then changes from those doctrinal positions after he is on the faculty. The honorable thing for a teacher to do if he no longer holds those doctrines is to resign and move on to a job where he fits, rather than staying on in the school and causing dissension. When you disagree with the school's doctrine, it is wrong to say that you have to obey God rather than man and stay in that school causing division and sowing discord among brethren. At that point, expect your services to be terminated.

Dedication

To be successful the school needs dedicated teachers. The

school cannot buy dedication as it does educational supplies and equipment. Dedication is the attitude of the teacher who approaches his work as a ministry.

Two people expressed their dedication to their work in simple sentences. One said, "Sir, this is not my work, it is my life." The other said upon retirement after 31 years at the same school, "I have accepted this school as my life's work." Those expressions are deep, giving insight into the meaning of genuine dedication. It is a matter of the heart.

Church Membership and Involvement

The school's purpose is to work in close harmony with the gospel-preaching church. Teachers should be members in good standing of sound churches. Spiritual nurture through school devotions and through the fellowship of the other teachers and staff should never become a substitute for such nurture in the church. The quality of fellowship in the school tends to be higher than that found in the church because all of the teachers are dedicated, spiritual Christians, a more select group than the church. School teachers spend more time together during the year striving for common goals than they do with other church members.

The Christian school teacher will have to determine how deeply to be involved in Sunday School teaching and youth work in the church. Our big ministry is the school. A teacher who does not feel that sense of priority should leave the school and serve God as a Christian education director in a church. It is not possible to give the school and the church equal priority. That is too much for one person no matter how gifted. Neither work will be done well.

Some teachers who serve in the church ask to teach a different age group from that of their school class. They find this variety stimulating. Others teach the same age and are happy. Some teach adults and find a carryover from that in working with the parents of their students.

It is particularly strenuous for a school teacher who is a married woman to be involved in a church ministry. If she has children, the matter is more intensified. Wives carry heavy responsibility for their husbands, their children, and their homes, and frequently it is all they can do to teach school. They need weekends and evenings for their families. It is not a sign of weakness, and a wife should not feel guilty if she serves God in the school and not in the church. Sometimes church people do not understand this, but they do not understand the rigors of daily school teaching plus the care of the family. Most people who are not educators really feel that school teachers do not work very hard. We know that is not true, even though others think so.

Students and parents are encouraged when teachers are members of their church. This helps to build positive attitudes in the students toward the church. Those attitudes are very important for Christian school students. If they are negative toward the church — turned off — they will leave the church when they become independent. That is tragic. It is so important for the Christian school teacher to speak favorably about the church, not only on Sunday but during the school week, and to encourage students to be involved in the church as long as they live. The church is of God and is for His people.

Support of Home and Foreign Missions

One of the things which attends solid Bible teaching over a period of years is this: God calls some of the hearers to take the gospel to people who have not heard, in America and in foreign countries. It is not the responsibility of the Christian school teacher to do this calling among his students for that is God's work. It is the responsibility of the teacher to be encouraging and supportive of home and foreign missions.

Over a period of years it will be your deep joy to see God leading some of your students to serve Him in a particular way at home and overseas. There will be surprises, for some that you could not predict will become His faithful servants in the bonds of Christ. Your joy will be further expressed by your prayers and by your financial help to these former students.

The Difference Between
Biblical Standards and Cultural Practices

The Christian school teacher must be a student of the Bible's standards. Confusion comes when a teacher somehow seems to equate cultural practices with biblical standards and begins to impose those cultural practices with the same force as the biblical standards. This does not imply that it is wrong to teach cultural practices. The point is that they should never be put on the same high level as Scripture. To illustrate, the question "What saith the Scripture?", is never to be equated with the question "What saith our cultural practices?"

Cultural practices are open to question and to revision. Biblical standards are not open to question and revision. They are absolutes, settled forever. This is not bad, for they are for our own good, for our very best.

Faithful, Hearty Work

Serving God in the school is a full-time job, and more. A teacher cannot be touchy about time, doing only what is required. A school whose teachers fulfill only the minimum requirements will not become an excellent school. A teacher needs to do more than what is required simply because he loves God and is giving all of his life to Him.

Above all, the teacher is directly responsible to the Lord for the work He has entrusted to the teacher. In certain areas and at certain times the teacher is very much on his own as far as human supervision goes, and has the privilege of seeking and finding the will of God. This means doing things heartily as to the Lord and not to man. The teacher who works harder when the principal is nearby is a man-pleaser and does not understand what it is to do all things heartily as to the Lord.

Enjoying God and His Goodness

Christian school teaching is a good life, a happy way to serve God. True, there are many problems, but that is so in every career. An overly intense, fretful, crabby Christian school teacher is not the representative that Christ needs in the classroom.

Your students will learn so much from you personally quite apart from your formal teaching. They need to see that you are enjoying God, that you are happy, that you are fulfilled in serving Him. They need to see an exemplary Christian.

During your teaching career you will go through some extremely dark days of heavy hearted tragedy both in your personal life and in the life of the school. In those periods, too, your students need to see that your confidence in God is unshaken even though you are crying and have a broken heart. At those times you communicate more to them about trusting God than you could in a whole report period of teaching your Bible lessons.

Respecting Spiritual Views of Parents

There are bound to be some differences between the teacher and some of the parents in areas which are not spelled out in the school's doctrinal statement. When those differences arise, the teacher is not free to proselyte the student to his viewpoint. Rather, the student should be told to discuss that item with his father and with his pastor. Of course the teacher can express his own viewpoint, but he may not press the student to adopt it. Again, this is not referring to the doctrinal platform of the school where the teacher should press the student to accept those beliefs.

The Christian school teacher can have a unifying influence in teaching students how to get along with other people who are truly Christian, but who hold differing ideas in some areas which are not related to the fundamental, essential, doctrines. Christians need help in learning how to get along with one another. This is not referring to heretics or apostates, but to Christians who do not see everything exactly the same way as the teacher.

Using All Talents

Most schools need teachers who are versatile and who are willing to use all of their talents in the ministry of the school. Expect all of your abilities to be exercised and do not take the position when you are asked to help out with something that you were not hired to do. You were hired to serve God with every capacity that you have.

Do not look at other teachers and feel that you are doing more than they because they may not be qualified to help out with such things as athletics, music, or drama in addition to their academic assignments. It is never possible to equalize the workload of every teacher. To whom much is given much is required, and you must accept the fact that some teachers are asked to do more than others. If you are called to do this, take it as from the Lord and give it your best sustained effort. There will be blessing in it for you if you accept it in the right spirit without contention in your heart. Teaching requires that you be a sacrificial giver of yourself on behalf of your students.

Personal Spiritual Retreats

Giving yourself to others is exhausting. To sustain yourself spiritually, you must come aside and rest for a while. Daily quiet time is essential in this regard, but longer periods of spiritual retreat for renewal are necessary. Uninterrupted time is needed to reflect, to be comforted, to think and pray through matters, to plan for the future, to get a clearer vision of your work, to understand Scripture and, above all, to know God. It is easier to be a doer than to be a thinker. The teacher should be both.

Respect for the Principal
and the Board

Authority is established by God, and in your ministry you are under the principal and the school board. Much of God's guidance for you will come through their decisions. Respect them, pray for them, honor them in the Lord for their work's sake.

Do not gossip and murmur about the principal or the board in the faculty room. If you disagree with the principal, speak directly to him about the matter, but do not cause disunity in the body by complaining to others. That critical spirit will grieve the Holy Spirit and the work of the school in the hearts of its students will not be as effective as it should be.

Sometimes a disrespectful, critical-spirited teacher thinks that no one would ever know that he has had such an attitude and tries to cover it up. The cover-up may work briefly, but soon that teacher is deceived into thinking no one else knows. A critical spirit cannot be concealed.

If you get into a murmuring attitude and cannot get the victory over the matter, the honorable thing is to resign from the school and ask God to place you in a school where you can respect the principal and the board. If you do that and still find yourself with a critical heart toward your new principal and new board, the problem probably lies with you and not with the administration. Instead of moving quickly to a third school, come to grips with yourself before the Lord. Consider also whether or not teaching is right for you. You might be better off in another occupation.

Embarrassing Colleagues

There is a lot of give and take among the members of a vigorous, creative faculty. Everyone will not see eye-to-eye, and there must be the freedom to be expressive of differences and of disagreements. This is healthy. It is low-key dynamic tension which keeps everyone thinking and talking without feeling like an insecure member of the group.

In this freedom there is always the potential for some problems. For example, an aggressive teacher can put another teacher or an administrator in an awkward position by pushing too far with a difference or disagreement before the entire faculty. Frequently it is the way the teacher says things, the tone of the voice and the facial expressions, as well as what he says that become hurtful. Be vigorous, disagree, speak out, but be discreet and do not cross the boundary line where you embarrass another publicly. Speak privately to the teacher or administrator where you have a strong difference, but do not precipitate a grievance situation by your behavior before the entire group.

Humility

The chances are that you liked school when you were in high school and college, and that is one reason that you studied to be a teacher. You were probably an above average student. Perhaps you were also an athlete, a musician, or a student leader. You may have won some awards during student days.

It is important that you not be proud and that you not brag about your accomplishments. The Bible says that it is God who works in us both to will and to do of His good pleasure. He is the vine and we are the branches. We are nothing, for although one plants and another waters, it is God who gives the increase. Let another person praise you but not your own lips.

This self-effacing humility was illustrated at the commencement of a Christian college. One of the alumni was honored for exceptional service to the Lord. He was called to the platform, and the college president read several typewritten pages of citations. When the citations were completed the audience applauded, and the alumnus stepped to the microphone to respond. His words were brief: "I have made it the practice of my life that He must increase and I must decrease. Thank you for this honor." That is all he said. He accepted the award graciously and sat down. The effect on the graduates and the audience was visible. They had just had spiritual contact with humility, and they knew it.

A Forgiving Spirit

The teacher needs to have a forgiving heart. This means to forgive and to forget. Our relationships with our colleagues and with our students and their parents are so close that there are always things happening that could offend us. Proverbs says that it is the glory of a man to overlook a transgression. The teacher who does not forgive and forget will carry grudges and will not have a good teaching experience even though he is in the Christian school.

Handling Complaints

Questions and complaints arise inevitably even in a well-run school. It is important that these be handled courteously, politely, and promptly. The following steps are an application of the Biblical injunction recorded in Matthew 18 for the resolution of a problem between believers:

1. The teacher meets privately with the parent to seek the resolution, with a spirit of reconciliation. Both want the good of the child and are not in an adversary position.
2. If unresolved, the teacher then meets with the parent and a third party, the principal.
3. If still unresolved, the matter is presented to the school board's education committee. The committee calls upon the parties involved as seems warranted, all in the spirit of reconciliation.
4. If still unresolved, the problem is brought before the entire school board. The board calls upon the parties involved as seems warranted, still in the spirit of reconciliation. If reconciliation still does not occur, the board makes the judgment as to who is wrong and takes appropriate disciplinary action against that person.

The principle underlying this procedure is clear: Solve each complaint with the persons directly involved at the lowest level possible, moving the matter up the chain of command to the level where it is finally resolved. The steps for handling a complaint about another teacher or administrator are exactly the same.

Spiritual Honesty

Sometimes a Christian school teacher gives the impression that he has no problems, he seems almost super-human. Students have trouble identifying with a teacher like that. As long as we are in this body, we are not going to be perfect. The teacher who pretends not to have any problems is presenting a distorted view of victorious Christian living. Victorious living does not mean that there are no problems. It means that God can meet those problems.

This does not mean that the teacher should tell his class all of his personal problems as a kind of confessional. The teacher should not wear his heart on his sleeve in that manner. What is needed is an honest spirit. For example, the Bible is written in a completely honest tone. Even David, years after killing Goliath, said that there were times when he was afraid. In Psalm 56:3 he said that in those times of fear he would trust the Lord. We identify with that; it touches our hearts, for we are like that. David would have given a false view and would not be our teacher if he had not been honest enough to say that there were times that he was afraid, but that in those times he trusted God.

A Maturing Christian

Christian school teachers need a youthful spirit. At the same time they need to be maturing in Christ. An interesting thing is always happening with the teacher. It is this: Over the years while he is teaching his students, God is teaching him concurrently. This is a wondrous thing, to teach others and to be taught yourself all at the same time. It is a distinctive blessing of our profession to be in the position of teacher and student simultaneously.

As teachers, we need to be soft-hearted toward God, very open to all that He says to us through His Word and by His Holy Spirit. Being teachable is a mark of a quality Christian school teacher. As the years go by we must come to know God better and better, understanding His Word all the more clearly, seeing all of life as sacred.

One nice thing about teaching is that you get a fresh start at the beginning of each school year. If we are maturing in Christ, each year we will be a better teacher than we were last year. When that is happening, our students are getting instruction that is more enriched than what we were able to give our students last year. We find ourselves enjoying teaching more and more rather than less and less, for we are more creative and have clearer insights because of our growth in the Lord. Teaching remains a great joy to us; and we do it as the natural expression of our love for God, not as a pleasant way to earn a living.

Teaching Values

Each day you will be teaching values by your own life before your students. Students do not talk about this, and perhaps they do not realize it, but they watch their teachers. Two things are going on all of the time in the classroom: academic learning and the learning of values. It is essential that you have a redeemed value system rather than a worldly value system.

There is much talk about values in the field of education today. Secular educators say that we should teach students how to determine values, but we should not tell the student what those values should be. This is not the teaching of the Scriptures, for God tells us what our values ought to be. To express it another way, we get our values from God's revelation. Secular educators seek their values from man's reason.

The way a teacher thinks about God, about man, and about the universe establishes the basic framework for his philosophy of life, for his standards of values, for his lifestyle. We have the spiritual insight to know that the existential philosophy, whose pervading theme is the meaninglessness and absurdity of all existence, is false. Its concept that the only purpose left in life is to eat, drink, and be merry for tomorrow we die, is wrong. The numerous philosophies of the world are lively and actively seek to entrap our students. They need to see in us a godly pattern, a practical example of the Bible's teaching in real life.

One of St. Paul's teaching methods was an appeal for Christians to watch him and copy the values which they saw in his life. He said:

> Those things, which ye have both learned, and received, and heard, and seen in me, do: and the God of peace shall be with you. Philippians 4:9
>
> Be ye followers of me, even as I also am of Christ. I Corinthians 11:1
>
> Brethren, be followers together of me, and mark them which walk so as to have us for an example. Philippians 3:17

A godly school teacher whose life is an example to his students is of great worth. Great damage is done by those teachers whose lives are a wrong example before impressionable children during the plastic years when their values, which will affect eternity, are being formed.

Helping With Chapel

Chapel periods are important in the life of the school. They are like family times when students and teachers alike come into a spiritual bond to praise and to worship God together. In some ways this is similar to the family altar at home.

From time to time you will be asked to participate in chapel. Always take that seriously, for the quality of chapel is important. Do not treat it lightly, and avoid the tendency to become mechanical, thinking that this is just another chapel. Each time it must be fresh, vital, alive. One chapel has the potential to influence a student's life as long as he lives. Think about that.

If you are asked to speak, wait on the Lord and bring a warm-hearted message from His Word. Emphasis should be placed upon the Scriptures, while using frequent true experiences to illustrate the scriptural truths which you are communicating. Never, never use the chapel as a time to blast the administration or the board. It is the place to direct attention to God, not to upset people by some diatribe.

Usually your contribution to a successful chapel will be in a support role. Be sure each student has his Bible. Get your class in the mood for worship by having them under control. Seat your students so that the talkers will be controlled. Pray quietly as chapel is in progress for God's work in hearts.

Chapels will be more meaningful to you if you approach them with the belief that God will surely minister to your heart as well as to the hearts of your students. You will be blessed if you come to chapel with an expectant heart for yourself as well as a prayerful heart for others. In His wondrous versatility, the Holy Spirit can minister to us teachers and to our students at one and the same time through the same music, through the same testimonies, and through the same message. You will miss this if you have the attitude that chapel is only for the students.

Instant In Season and Out Of Season

Although in school work efforts are made to plan ahead, it sometimes happens that you will be asked to minister spiritually to a class or to a chapel on extremely short notice. Do not panic, for that short-noticed opportunity will be a fine experience for you in knowing the Lord's leading in a practical way. You will find yourself trusting God very hard, and that is good. He knows that you did not have advance notice and that it is not your fault that you did not prepare. He will help, for He is a very present help in time of trouble.

There are some practical suggestions that may help you when this happens. Each suggestion assumes that you are praying for God's help even as you think of what to say. The first suggestion is this: Give your personal testimony showing how God saved you, how He has guided you, and some of His clear working in your life. Students will identify with an honest, ungarnished testimony. It will help them to know you better spiritually.

Second, give a short devotional from one of your favorite portions of Scripture. Use a portion that you read frequently in your own quiet time because you are so blessed by it. Do not be concerned if it is a well-known portion. If it has deep meaning to you, you will be able to present it in a warmhearted way and will communicate to others some of God's precious personal lessons to you. This approach is always blessed by God, for there is a tone of deep sincerity and earnestness that comes through in the talk. People sense that you really mean what you are saying, and the Spirit uses that to impress those Scriptures upon the hearts of the listeners. To illustrate, some of your own favorite portions of the Word were probably taught to you by persons to whom that portion was also a favorite.

Third, share a verse or a passage from the Bible that God has recently made significant to your life through your own devotions or through a sermon. Part of the marvel of the inspiration of the Bible is the way in which the Holy Spirit emphasizes certain verses to us just at the time that we have a definite need in our lives for that particular truth. It may well be a Scripture that you have known for years, but it is very strong to you now because of your current life situation. You can speak on a passage like that quite effectively, because you are appropriating it in your personal life right now.

Do not disintegrate when you are asked to speak with no prior notice. It is an opportunity from the Lord. If you turn it down, that exact opportunity will not come to you again. If you accept it, God will help you in a remarkable way. Try it.

Giving Money To The School

There is blessing in giving some of your tithes and offerings to the school. It is true that you are already giving to the school by accepting a contract that is less than what you would earn at a secular school. At the same time, your school needs gift money in addition to the tuition the parents pay to balance the annual operating budget and to finance capital improvements. Give some of your money as well as your life, for you belong to the school body and it needs money.

The Lord loves a cheerful giver. It is also His way to give without fanfare. You are giving it to Him, not to the board, or not even to your students. Let it be a private matter between you and God. If you do it privately and unpretentiously, He will bless you openly. God is no man's debtor. It does not make sense to give God your life at the school, but not give Him any of your money there.

Handling Judgment By Others

It is our responsibility to follow close after the Lord, as a servant follows his master. We need to know His approval or disapproval. Frequently He uses people to show us this, but we must look beyond them to recognize Him. "Whatsoever He saith unto you, do it," is the principle by which we teach. Teachers get all kinds of judgment, and it is so important to discern what is of God.

When we know that we are pleasing God, we should not be unduly concerned about the praise or about the blame of man. This concept was expressed by the apostle Paul in I Corinthians 4 when he said that with him it was a very small thing that he should be judged of man's judgment. He said that he was judged by the Lord. Living like this gave him great emotional stability to endure the severe problems that came to him so frequently. If he had made his decisions on the basis of man's judgment rather than on the basis of God's judgment, he would not have become the exemplary Christian that he is to us and he would not have had such a successful ministry of service to God and to man.

Comparison With Others

In teaching there is a natural tendency to compare ourselves with other members of the faculty in different ways. This is a subtle thing and should be avoided. Our performance before the Lord should never be thought of in comparative terms with that of another teacher. The question is this: How well am I performing in comparison with the way that I am capable of performing? We have to give it our very best.

Solomon put it this way in Ecclesiastes 9:10, "Whatsoever thy hand findeth to do, do it with thy might . . ." Paul said a similar thing in Colossians 3:23, 24, "And whatsoever ye do, do it heartily, as to the Lord, and not unto men; knowing that of the Lord ye shall receive the reward of the inheritance: for ye serve the Lord."

Comparison with others may encourage us or it may discourage us. Either is wrong, for you are unique, and God wants you to be the teacher He means you to be without evaluating your performance in comparison with others. Obviously He wants you to do well. If you do not, do not expect to be rehired next year. But, be your own person, and develop all of your abilities to their fullest. God has given you the gift of teaching by His Holy Spirit. Exercise it.

Apologizing When Necessary

There are times when we are wrong, and we must apologize for whatever we have done or for whatever we left undone. This must be done even though the teacher is in the place of authority. An apology is not a sign of weakness. It is a mark of a strong character. Although it is embarrassing, it is wholesome to you and to the others.

God has a way of using your heart-felt and simple apology to actually strengthen your relationship with the student, with the class, with your fellow-teacher, with the administrator, or with the parent, to whom you must apologize. You would think it would cause a breach, for you were wrong; but what it does is to bring healing. It will sensitize your heart, too, by keeping your conscience clear before the Lord; for you know you are right with your fellow man.

Do not try to bluff your way out of the situation. Give a clear, direct apology and keep pressing ahead. Then do not brood over your mistakes. Apologize, and move ahead in your ministry to your students.

Two Sides to Every Story

Christian school teaching is so interesting because there is always something happening. With all of this action, the teacher is called upon daily to make decisions or to give an opinion. When this happens, it is important not to make up your mind and not to say anything until you have taken the time to get all of the facts on both sides of the story. A quick, impetuous decision or opinion is hurtful.

The teacher can always retract what he said before he had all of the information. That does not erase the fact that he said it, and students are good at remembering what the teacher said in this situation. Train yourself to be restrained in your judgment of a matter until you have both sides, even though there may be a clamor for you to do something or to say something immediately.

The counsel of Solomon on this point fits us teachers well. In Proverbs 18:13 he said, "He that answereth a matter before he heareth it, it is folly and shame unto him." This is also God's counsel, for He inspired Solomon to write those words.

A Guard Upon the Lips

To quote Solomon again, "He who guards his mouth and his tongue guards his soul from troubles," Proverbs 21:23; and, "In the multitude of words there wanteth not sin: but he that refraineth his lips is wise," Proverbs 10:19.

To teach we must talk a great deal. There is a difference between instructional talking and the talking of which the

Word cautions us. It seems reasonable that those who have to talk a lot in their work might be susceptible to also talking a lot in the wrong way. At those points the Christian school teacher must set a guard upon his lips.

Talk that is gossip, murmuring, maligning, or complaining displeases God. Somehow that kind of talk appeals to us from time to time. It is very engrossing. We may even encourage one another in it in the faculty room, for it is easy to get it going. It is hard to stop it.

Teachers know a great deal of information about parents, students, homes, administrators, etc. The teacher must realize that he is a trustee of this information. It does not really belong to him but to those people, so he is not free to spread it, to use it indiscriminately. Talking about students and people in the school must be upon the highest professional level, and then kept strictly within the faculty. There are many times when such talk is in order, for it is necessary to understand and to help a student or a family. Again, all such discussion must be kept in confidence, as medical doctors protect the confidentiality of their patients' physical problems.

Control of Temper

An ill temper, a short fuse, is not suitable for a Christian school teacher. The teacher's testimony for Christ is hurt dramatically if he loses his temper in the classroom, at a ball game, or in a faculty meeting. There are strong pressures upon the teacher, and he must look to God for His help in self-control.

Thinking again from the book of Proverbs — and that book says so much of a practical nature to teachers — God says, "The discretion of a man deferreth his anger; and it is his glory to pass over a transgression," Proverbs 19:11. In chapter 16, verse 32, of the same book, God tells us, "He that is slow to anger is better than the mighty; and he that ruleth his spirit than he that taketh a city."

Self-control is a fruit of the Holy Spirit in our lives, an

evidence of His work in us, according to Galatians. The wrath of man does not work the righteousness of God. Paul told Timothy that the servant of the Lord must not strive, but be gentle unto all men, apt to teach, patient, in meekness instructing those that oppose themselves. There is no place for a hot temper in the Christian school teacher.

A Little Folly

A good, hearty, sense of humor goes a long way in Christian school teaching. It is wholesome for the teacher and for the students. It helps to make education fun. It brightens the day and makes time go faster. It adds to the faculty meeting.

By contrast, a little folly in the life of the teacher is out of place. It takes a lifetime to build a personal testimony, but it can be torn down in one day. The teacher must be above reproach in all areas of life. God says to abstain from all appearance of evil. Folly disqualifies us from the Christian School profession. Every year there are teachers who lose their jobs because of folly.

The book of Ecclesiastes talks about the matter of a little folly in an unusually graphic way. In chapter 10, verse 1, the Word of God puts it like this, "Dead flies cause the ointment of the apothecary to send forth a stinking savour: so doth a little folly him that is in reputation for wisdom and honor."

Draw a clear line between humor and folly, and then stay well back from the folly side. Do not see how close you can come to folly without getting burned. "Avoid it, pass not by it, turn from it, and pass away," Proverbs 4:15. Your students do not need dead flies in the life of their teacher.

Resist the Devil

It is not crying, "Wolf, wolf," to say that the devil is actively opposing the school where you teach. It is not an exaggeration to warn you that he also is actively opposing you personally. When a work becomes aggressive and effective for God, those workers must be prepared for the machinations of Satan.

The admonition in James 4:7 must be appropriated daily, "Submit yourselves therefore to God. Resist the devil, and he will flee from you." A teacher who does not do this is simply out of touch with spiritual reality, and does not understand the nature of the work. Christian school teaching is great; but it is a battle, a warfare, every day between the forces of the evil one and the power of God. Teachers must have their eyes open to this fact, must be always on the alert.

Satan's involvement in the educational program of the school is expressed in an interesting way by Dr. E. William Male, Founder of the National Institute of Christian School Administration, Director of the graduate program in Christian School Administration, Dean of Grace Theological Seminary. Dr. Male says, "Satan pitched his tent under the tree of knowledge in the garden of Eden at the beginning of civilization, and he hasn't moved it yet."

We teachers do not fear Satan, for we know that greater is He — Christ — who is in you than he who is in the world — Satan. At the same time, we must realize that the weapons to be used against him are not our graduate degrees in education or our years of experience in the classroom. If we battle him with those weapons, he will eat us up every time.

The Bible is clear in telling us how to resist the devil in Ephesians 6:10-18. God says,

> Finally, my brethren, be strong in the Lord, and in the power of his might. Put on the whole armour of God, that ye may be able to stand against the wiles of the devil. For we wrestle not against flesh and blood, but against principalities, against powers, against the rulers of the darkness of this world, against spiritual wickedness in high places. Wherefore take unto you the whole armour of God, that ye may be able to withstand in the evil day, and having done all, to stand. Stand therefore, having your loins girt about with truth, and having on the breastplate of righteousness; And your feet shod with the preparation of the gospel of peace; Above all taking the shield of faith, wherewith ye shall be able to quench all the fiery darts of the wicked. And take the helmet of salvation, and the sword of the Spirit, which is the word of God: Praying always with all prayer and supplication in the Spirit, and watching thereunto with all perseverance and supplication for all saints.

Chapter Two

PRACTICAL
ACADEMIC CONCERNS

No child or young person should have to take an academic penalty in order to get a Christian education. The school is Christian, but it is a school. Good teachers are serious about their responsibility to give their students a quality education. It is a sobering thought to realize that the work of a teacher will affect the next fifty or sixty years of a child's life, if the Lord tarries, and if he lives to a full age of threescore years and ten. Excellence in education benefits the student and it honors the name of Christ in the community. As a teacher, do not aim at being a good teacher; rather seek to excel for God.

Personal In-Service Growth

A Christian school teacher must continue to grow academically after finishing college in the way that a medical doctor must continue to grow professionally after he completes medical school. This growth does not occur quickly. It must be carefully planned or it will not come about.

Personal in-service growth involves a teacher's evaluation of himself, and a plan for overcoming his weaknesses. It is good to make an annual self-evaluation and then revise the in-service plan as warranted. Every year progress is being made, and every year more progress is outlined.

Do not try to accomplish more than is reasonable in a one year period. Accept the fact that you are always going to have areas in which you want to improve, establish priorities, and work patiently at becoming a more competent teacher. Keep working faithfully and over a period of years you will develop into a strong Christian school teacher. Faithfulness is a key. Do not allow long periods of time to go by when you are not improving yourself.

In some schools the principal will work with you in evaluation and in the personal in-service plan. This is helpful because it brings another viewpoint into the matter. The Bible says that in the multitude of counselors there is wisdom. Together you will have a better evaluation and a better plan. If your principal does not do this, do it on your own. Make it the practice of your life to evaluate and improve, evaluate and improve. That is the nature of your occupation.

Annual Goals

As you teach this year, you will see places where you could have done a better job. Keep a file folder for next year, because then you will have another opportunity. During the summer, after you are rested, review the notes in the folder and establish reasonable goals for improving your performance this year. Devise plans for reaching those goals. In this way, each year your new students will be getting improved instruction over last year. Do this concurrently with your personal in-service program. Annual goals are more immediate and are easier to accomplish.

When working on your in-service program and when establishing annual goals, take time to commit these important matters to God, asking for His help. The procedures suggested can be followed profitably by any teacher, but only the saved teacher can also get God's viewpoint upon his plans. He says in Isaiah 55:7, 8, "For my thoughts are not your thoughts, neither are your ways my ways, saith the

Lord. For as the heavens are higher than the earth, so are my ways higher than your ways, and my thoughts than your thoughts." This works. The spiritual approach to any matter is always practical.

Earning the Master's Degree

It should be part of your personal in-service program to earn your master's degree. Perhaps you should do advanced work beyond the master's. The master's is the place to start, the first goal.

First and second year teachers usually have their hands full with their work and are not in a position to add the burdens of graduate school to the present load. Use those first years to think seriously about the field in which you want to earn your degree and investigate the graduate schools offering that program, for all are not equally good. You do not want the degree just to have a master's, you want it to make you a better teacher. Enroll in the best program you can find.

During the years that you are in graduate school, those studies must have priority. Other activities have to be cut back so the degree can be completed. This requires a teacher to be disciplined. It is part of paying the full price. Go into the program with a commitment to complete it. If a thesis is required, get to it and finish it. Do not be satisfied with anything less. You do not want to say for years to come that you finished everything for your master's but . . .

Be sure to study the federal income tax laws when you are doing graduate work. It is possible that much of your educational expenses would be deductible. It would be worth the money to talk the matter through with a qualified tax consultant or with a representative of IRS.

Educational Seminars and Conventions

Short-term conventions, seminars, and institutes are worthwhile experiences for professional growth. Many Christian schools participate in state or regional Christian school conventions. The major addresses and the workshops help Christian teachers to see things from the Christian viewpoint. They also give practical help. In addition, the fellowship with others from your own faculty, and the fellowship with teachers from other Christian schools is uplifting. The conventions give a feeling of cohesion, an appreciation of the fact that we are part of the greatest educational program in the world, "God's School System."

To get the most out of a convention, stay at the hotel with the other delegates, attend the banquet, eat with the other delegates. You will miss out if you stay overnight with friends in the community and eat fast food instead of the banquet in an effort to save a few dollars. Spend the money and get the full impact of the convention.

Numerous secular educational organizations also sponsor high quality conventions, seminars, and institutes. It is good to be involved in the ones related to your teaching field, even though they do not include the spiritual dimension. It is helpful to approach a secular convention with this frame of mind: This conference offers me knowledge, even though it does not offer me spiritual wisdom or understanding. Take that knowledge and handle it in the framework of Biblical presuppositions. Do not take the position that you cannot learn anything as a Christian school teacher from a person who is not a Christian. That narrow view upon education is stifling. Draw the distinction between knowledge and spiritual wisdom and understanding.

Membership in Professional Organizations

Membership in Christian School organizations and membership in other professional organizations in your field of teaching are both helpful. This keeps the teacher informed of current trends in education. It keeps him posted on new books in his field. It tells him of regional and local meetings. It tells him of speakers and seminars.

It is particularly helpful when a professional organization has a local chapter which meets periodically to hear a top speaker and to have an interchange of ideas. Christian school teachers should not draw back from such involvement. You are part of the educational world. True, your philosophy of education is completely different, but you are a bonafide professional educator. Interplay with other educators in the same field will teach you things, and will sharpen your own convictions, helping you to be a more refined educator in your Christian school ministry. Be professional, do not back away.

Professional Reading

Strong teachers are usually readers themselves. This would include professional magazines, journals and books. Every article is not equally important. Some articles and chapters of books should be skimmed, while others should be read in depth. If one or two good ideas can be gained from an article or from a chapter, that reading has been very valuable.

It is well to have a personal program for reading. Some teachers read one book a month, and several professional magazines. This reading is in addition to devotional reading and recreational reading.

Many schools have a professional library. Teachers can request that certain magazines be purchased. They can also request the purchase of selected professional books. A few schools give the teachers an annual allotment of money to spend on their own professional magazines and books. If the school does not have either of these plans, the teacher must budget money out of his own pocket to buy these things. It is too important a matter to let it go just because the school does not pay for it as a fringe benefit.

Thinking further about money, many schools provide fringe benefits to help the professional development of the teacher. These benefits include tuition help for graduate work as long as that program is related to your assignment at the school, expenses to educational conferences and seminars, membership in professional organizations, and professional magazines and books. Some schools cannot afford this, and some pay only a portion of the expenses. If you work in such a school it will be harder on you, but you must trust God and work to get the money to finance your professional development. It must be done, even when it is hard to accomplish because the school does not provide it. God will help you in this, for you are doing it for Him.

Professional Visitation Days

Once or twice a year it is good to leave the classroom, get away from the campus, and visit a master teacher in another school who teaches the same grade or the same subject that you do. This observation is stimulating and ideas can be brought back to your own responsibilities.

Careful planning should go into a day like this to get the most out of it. Permission from your principal to be out on that day should be secured several weeks in advance. So should permission from the teacher whom you want to visit. Plan to spend the full day with the other teacher. Arrive early to talk a bit before classes begin, and stay after school is dismissed to raise questions or to ask for clarification. During the day be unobtrusive and very careful not to interrupt the work of the teacher with the class. This experience is so valuable that all teachers, veterans, middlers, and beginners can learn from it.

Service on Accreditation Visiting Committees

Teachers who work in accredited Christian schools are invited periodically by the accrediting agency to serve on visitation committees which must go to other schools for the purpose of evaluating that school for accreditation. This is one of the most worthwhile experiences that a Christian school teacher can have. It is a rigorous experience, not a vacation, taking two to three days.

Several interesting things happen simultaneously during those days. Evaluating other teachers and the other school within the guidelines of the evaluation criteria of the accrediting association is a quality experience in careful evaluation. Writing clear commendations and recommendations to the school is a good professional exercise. Understanding the accreditation process more clearly because of this high level involvement helps you when your own school is up for accreditation, for you have been through it. The most interesting result is this: As you evaluate the other school, you find yourself thinking about your own school and how it compares with this school. You return to your own school after the two or three day visit with a valid list of improvements which should be introduced as possible.

Do not turn down an invitation to serve on a visiting team for an accreditation agency unless you are under an emergency situation in your life. It is worth more than a graduate course, more than a convention, and more than reading several good books.

Lesson Planning

Administrators differ in the lesson planning which they require of teachers. Some require that the plans for next week be submitted to the office by Friday afternoon. Others require that the teacher have an up-to-date plan book in his desk. Still others require none of the above.

No matter what requirements are upon you, it is true that good teaching comes from good planning. Good planning comes from unhurried, reflective thinking about the needs of the class and about the subject matter to be covered. Good teachers take time after they have taught to write comments on their plans as to how they could have been better. The next time around they incorporate these improvements.

Trusting the Lord for His hand upon us while we teach does not mean that we should not plan. Plan as carefully as you can, yet be flexible as the lesson proceeds. Stay on the track of the lesson while staying free to discuss things that come up within the boundaries of that track. There will be some spontaneous matters that lend themselves to a superlative teaching situation. The general rule, however, is that quality teaching occurs when there has been prayerful, quality planning in advance.

Pre-School Orientation

A good start helps to set the tone for the new year. The pre-school orientation days should not be approached as a drag, but as an opportunity for spiritual fellowship with the faculty and staff and as a professional learning experience. It is a warm-up period, not a giving up the end of vacation days period. The teacher approaching orientation with this positive attitude will have a good experience every year.

Orientation days usually give the teacher some free time to get his room and books ready to go. If the schedule does not permit this or if the orientation days are like a retreat held off-campus, you should plan to spend about two other days on your own in the building before opening day.

Be friendly to the new teachers at orientation. This is the time to begin to build relationships with them, the time to make them feel at home, the time to make them accepted as members of the body in full standing. A teacher's attitude toward his job is influenced the most by his feelings toward his immediate superior and toward his colleagues. This is one reason why the body life principles are so important within a Christian school.

Faculty Meeting

A teacher who approaches faculty meetings as an infringement upon his personal time does not get much from the meeting and is a negative influence upon the spirit of the meeting. The teacher who looks on the meeting as a time for fellowship, professional growth, and problem solving benefits personally and adds to others during the meeting.

Be involved in the meeting without monopolizing it. Do not be a spectator, but a participant. There is a kind of group intelligence, group creativity, and group wisdom when the faculty is together. You are part of that. Be innovative, be creative, share your insights.

Do not use the faculty meeting as a platform to lash out at a student, parent, or colleague. Approach discussions involving people as the professional educator that you are and keep your feelings under control. Discussing issues involving people should be handled as professionally as a group of medical consultants talking together about a patient's physical problems. Talk freely in the meeting, but then be careful not to talk about the discussion after the meeting is over with unauthorized personnel.

Time

Christian school teaching is not a job for a person who is a clock watcher. It frequently requires what some would call overtime. For the teacher, overtime is really normal time. After classes, there are meetings, special events, grading, planning, and so forth.

Learn to use your time efficiently. It is not to be squandered. Do not feel sorry for yourself and do not complain because you have a longer work day than your friends who have other occupations. Teaching is hard work.

Watch your attitude toward the other teachers. Do not be miffed when you are called upon to help with some extracurricular activity, probably without extra pay. Your time represents your life, and you have been called to serve God with your life at the school. A touchy attitude toward time will cut back your joy in your work.

Because teaching is so time consuming, good vacation periods are very important to you. Ask God to help you to plan and to finance vacations that will refresh you spiritually and physically. You need times of rejuvenation or you will run yourself into the ground and will be a burned-out teacher. There were times when even the Lord Jesus withdrew from people to be strengthened. He also told His disciples to come aside and rest for awhile. The Lord is able to provide those times for you.

Reporting to Parents

Reporting pupil progress to parents is a serious matter which must be done well. The school's standards for grading, and the school's forms for reporting to parents must be followed exactly. This is not a place for the teacher to be independent, to free-lance, because he does not quite agree with the school's system. Until the system is revised, the current one must be followed.

Parents and students read academic marks, character ratings, and report card comments carefully. Those marks, ratings, and comments must be absolutely accurate.

The teacher who releases inaccurate grades must be fair, recheck his calculations, and revise the grade. Every time this happens a shadow is cast upon the teacher's accuracy, upon his credibility, in fact, upon his very competence. If the teacher has made a few grading errors, the principal wonders if there are others which have gone undetected, to the detriment of the student and his parents.

Written comments on a report card or in a letter to parents must be grammatically correct and free of all spelling errors. For some reason, people expect teachers to be correct in their writing and in their spelling. Mistakes in these things are especially damaging to the professional reputation of the teacher. The reasoning is that if the teacher cannot do these things himself, how is he going to teach them to the students? You must proofread your report cards. It is helpful to have the principal or a fellow teacher also read your cards before they go out. It is far better for them to catch your mistake than to have it go to the parent incorrect.

Get a good start on your report cards whenever they are due for release. Do not allow a lot of grading of papers to pile up so that too much has to be done at the last minute. The chance of making mistakes increases when you are harried. Your written comments will be superficial and will tend to be similar rather than individualistic when you do not have the time to be reflective because you are hard pressed to meet the deadline. Plan your personal schedule carefully at the end of the report period to give yourself the extra time needed to do a quality job of preparing each student's report card.

Bulletin Board and Furnishings

Creative teachers use bulletin boards and homeroom furnishings as teaching aides. Colorful, thought-provoking displays and pictures liven the classroom atmosphere and stimulate students. A dull room is boring.

Some professional magazines carry a regular article suggesting a bulletin board for the month. There are also books on the market giving ideas for bulletin boards. Alert teachers always collect information, pictures, and articles for their personal files to be used on bulletin boards and in displays. Ideas for possible combinations should be filed for future use. A bulletin board may be years in planning.

There is a time value on bulletin boards and displays. They should be replaced when they have accomplished their purposes. When they are up too long they are no longer helpful and give the impression of a tired teacher.

Take advantage of the freedom in the Christian school to share Christ and biblical teachings by always having at least one or two items in your room which you could not have on display if you were teaching in a secular school. The Christian school classroom should be distinctively Christian, not just like a good secular school classroom. Often Christian school teachers do not do this, for they did their student teaching in public schools where they were not permitted to put up anything that was clearly Christian. To do the same in Christian school is great loss. Exercise your freedom. Give creative thought to being Christian in this area. Ask God for ideas. The results will surprise you.

Record Keeping

It is more satisfying to work with students in the classroom and in activities than to be doing the paperwork which is required of teachers. The records must be done, and done accurately. Be certain that you understand the records for which you are responsible. Learn the style of writing or of recording and follow the school's requirements.

Get the records done on time. Some can be started in advance, others cannot be started until a particular date has been reached. Reserve time in your personal schedule, get a good start, and enjoy the sense of relief when you finish that job. There are no short cuts, no tricks.

Parents have the right to see the records of their children upon request. This is nothing to fear. It does mean that records must be accurate, in good order, professional. Written comments must be capable of justification. Avoid all flip comments or impulsive words off the top of your head about a student. Records by a Christian school teacher should reflect wise, temperate evaluations, always with love and respect for the student.

Standardized Tests

Teachers like to know how their students are doing as compared with students in other schools. Standardized tests are some indication.

The individual Christian school should determine what tests it wants to give and the time of administration. Be thankful if your school has its tests machine scored. It is more likely that you will have to score them by hand and then compile all of the statistics, a tedious job which is guaranteed to reduce your social life during testing time. The results are of high interest.

There is wisdom in not bragging too much about your

school if the students score above the national norms on the standardized tests. There are two reasons for a subdued reaction. First, the students in the local public school may also score above the national norms. If you give the impression that because your students are above national norms they are above the local public schools, that may not be true. Second, Christian schools tend to be selective in admissions, which the public schools can not be. Since the Christian school students are average or above, it should be expected that their standardized test scores would come in above national norms.

Several major testing companies handle this distortion by publishing two sets of norms, one for public schools and another for independent schools. The norms for independent schools are considerably higher. Compared to independent school norms, many Christian schools are not as good academically as they think they are.

Students With Physical Needs

Check with the nurse before the opening day of school to find out which students have special physical needs. Occasionally a student may have a serious problem such as a heart condition, hemophilia, or a severe reaction to insect bites. You may have a student who is diabetic or epileptic. Others may have hearing problems or sight problems. Still others will have more apparent handicaps.

Talk with the parents and with the nurse to get the clearest understanding of the child. Be sure you know exactly what to do if the child has an emergency during the school day. Be prepared.

Confer with the prinicpal to be sure that he understands the particular problems of your class. Ask him to clarify your responsibilities for each student. Ask for a clear definition of your personal liability in handling each problem.

Check to make certain that the school carries liability insurance which covers you. If it does not, buy your own policy to cover your personal liability. This is not an expensive kind of insurance.

An admonition from Scripture is appropriate in this discussion. God says that we should watch and pray. While being prepared, pray that God will keep your students from serious problems. Even when problems occur, and they do even in a praying school, God has a way of restraining their severity compared to what could happen.

Activities and Injuries

Over the years accidents and injuries will occur. When they do, lift your heart to God, be courageous and cool. Send a reliable person for adult help immediately. As you minister to the student in need be extremely cautious remembering that you are not a medical doctor. Do only what a responsible person would do in such an emergency.

Caution may indicate a trip to the hospital by ambulance under medical supervision. The principal would make that decision.

Take a few minutes when you get back to your room to write out an anecdotal record of the matter. Note the date, the time, and the incident. Later you may be asked for these details by an insurance company, or even a lawyer, and they will fade from your memory as time passes. If your school has its own accident report form, be sure it is filed promptly with the nurse or with the principal. Be sure that the nurse and the principal, in particular, know what happened and how you handled it.

Follow-up with the child and his parents gives unusual opportunities to express your love. Phone calls, visits to the hospital, visits to the home, thoughtful gifts, all help to build wholesome spiritual relationships between you, the child, and the family. Getting the time to do these will disrupt your personal time schedule, but God knows that and He will bless you for putting yourself out to minister to this family in the time of their child's need. These happenings will intensify your understanding of Christian school teaching as a total ministry, not just a job.

This situation gives the opportunity to lead the children in the class to show love to their classmate. Through daily prayer, letters, and thoughtful gifts, the children can learn practical applications of Christian body-life principles.

Evaluate the accident to see whether or not it can be prevented from reoccuring. Perhaps it was caused by a physical object that can be changed. Perhaps it was caused by some lack of order on the part of the students, and a rule should be set to establish the order needed. Some accidents can not be prevented, but many can be and it is foolish not to take quick, firm measures to prevent the same thing from happening again. The physical health and safety of your children is an essential part of your responsibility as a Christian school teacher.

Playground, Bus, and Cafeteria Duty

Christian school students need continuous supervision by their teachers. Supervision is part of our ministry and must be done well. Duty on the playground, at the bus, or at the cafeteria, is not much fun, but it is more satisfying with a positive attitude than with a negative attitude. Accept it as a responsibility from the Lord, and do it as unto Him.

Be on time when it is your turn for duty. A tardy teacher leaves students unsupervised or puts extra responsibility on other teachers who are on time. It is not fair to avoid your share of duty. When you do not show or when you are late, you are foreseeably negligent and are liable for whatever happens in your absence. That is serious.

Duty times offer opportunities for strengthening relationships with students. The setting is more informal and relaxed than the classroom, and there is time to talk to students on a lighter level, and sometimes on a counseling level. The teacher who thinks that his work is the classroom and does his duty in a negative way is missing out and is unhappy.

Your classroom ministry is deeper when you enjoy the students and get to know them better while on duty.

Duties give a feeling for the school as a whole because you will have students from several classes under your care. You will be blessed when your former students talk to you and you see them maturing. The younger brothers and sisters of your students will also come to you, and you will get to know the family better. Always envision the whole school, and see yourself as a servant of Christ to every student with particular responsibility for your own class or classes.

Visitors

Think of visitors as opportunities, not as disruptions. If they are parents, a favorable impression may be the thing which persuades them to enroll their children in the school, and years of Christ-centered education will result. Be yourself, and help your class to be natural. It would be devious to put on airs, a performance, while visitors are in the room.

If it is possible, explain to the visitors what is going on in the class and give them materials to follow. Give them an opportunity to raise questions. Do this without losing the class. If big questions are asked, tell the visitor that you will be happy to answer when class is over, but you do not have time right now. Be candid.

When the principal or the department head comes to visit, proceed with the lesson as you normally would. Quietly ask God to keep you from being nervous, especially during an evaluation visit, and teach the lesson as planned. There is no need to freeze when an administrator visits. Some teachers rise to the occasion and teach better with visitors than when alone in the classroom. Perhaps you are like that. The Christian teacher realizes that God is always present in the classroom, so a few human visitors do not make much difference. We are not to fear man.

Student-Teachers

Be willing to accept an invitation from the principal to have a college senior as a student-teacher. The invitation means that the principal has confidence in you to prepare another teacher to enter the Christian school teaching profession. It will mean extra work for you, but God is no man's debtor and will reward you. Look on this as an unusual opportunity to reproduce yourself in the life of a future Christian school teacher.

The education professor of the sponsoring college will orient you for this experience. He will explain the requirements which the student-teacher must fulfill while at the school. He will probably give you a booklet explaining your role.

This is always a stimulating thing because you will find yourself thinking hard about your teaching, for you are now the model for a neophyte, a serious responsibility. One outcome is your own professional growth. Another outcome is the professional growth of the student-teacher. Long time friendships may develop between the two of you.

Student-teachers who feel called of God to teach in Christian schools are greatly helped by student teaching in a Christian school instead of a secular school. The experience gets them started on the right track in understanding the distinctive aims and objectives of Christian education. The secular school cannot help in this area.

All of us teachers had to start sometime, and we are indebted to those experienced teachers who accepted us as their student-teachers. For example, I continue to thank God for the influence of Marge Stockwell and Mary Ross, under whom I student taught in a Christian school. They charted the course for me, far more clearly than my education professors who did not understand why I wanted to teach in a Christian school. It seems logical for veteran teachers to help beginners.

New Faculty and Staff Members

Part of your ministry to the faculty-staff body is helping new personnel in their adjustments to their new school. Sometimes veterans forget what it was like to be a rookie at the school, and do not give the friendship and simple help that would make the transition of the new person so much easier and pleasant. If your school has a buddy system of pairing off a new teacher with a veteran, get involved in it.

Accept new personnel immediately as Christians and as colleagues. There is no room in the school for a caste system based upon longevity at the school, upon advanced degrees, or upon position. The concept of the group as a miniature of the body of Christ does not allow for that behaviour.

Student Career Guidance

Students who enjoy school very much should be challenged to pray about the possibility of becoming Christian school teachers. A few encouragements from you in this direction can be used of God to give direction to the student. This is a long-range thing which needs patient encouragement and prayer over a period of years. It is well worth the effort for the results are gratifying. It is wonderful to see your graduates teaching in Christian schools.

Teachers who graduated from Christian schools bring good insights to the faculty. They see things from the student vantage point as well as from the faculty viewpoint. This is like the missionary kid who becomes a missionary.

Above all, your own enthusiasm for Christian school teaching will stimulate certain students to consider your career field for their own. This is also true of coaches and of administrators. God uses people and His Word to show students His will for their lives.

Professionalism

Christian school teaching is a ministry but it is also a profession. We are professional educators, with all of the responsibilities which fall to professional people. It is important that we be professional in all of our teaching and in all of our dealings with people. We are not amateur teachers.

Some Christian school teachers have a poor self-image. They think too lowly of themselves. True, we are to be humble for everything we are is the result of God in our lives. Teachers must have a good self-image and humility at the same time. It is not true that if a person cannot make it in another job he can always become a Christian school teacher.

Professionalism speaks of quality, of excellence in education. We have the great joy of bearing the Lord's name in the field of education, for we teach in "God's School System". Our motivation to professional excellence stems from our heart's desire to honor Him, not from any desire of personal pride or personal gain.

God is honored when we teach at our capacity, exercising the gift of teaching which the Holy Spirit has given us to the fullest. Our commitment to Christ on behalf of our students is total. We are not experimenting with Christian education.

Chapter Three

RECOMMENDATIONS ABOUT SCHOOL ACTIVITIES

Christian school teaching encompasses the entire educational program of the school, not just the classroom. Activities are an integral part of a student's education. They are not a superfluous addend. Good schools have good activity programs. Quality programs do not just happen. They are planned and carried out by capable, conscientious, Christian school teachers.

The section which follows gives selected recommendations about the teacher's involvement, attitude, and approach to the activities of the school.

Supporting Activities

The teacher usually has to use his own free time to support student activities. This is a worthy investment of time, for God uses activities in a special way in building relationships with students. They know that the teacher is on his own time and take this as an indication that the teacher cares about them and about what they are doing. Teachers who support activities earn popularity and respect from the student body. This deepens their ministry with the students, for the students are more open to them.

It is easier to support the activities of your own greatest interest. This is not a wise approach, for students in the activities of your lesser interests are equally deserving of your time and attention. It is best to attend a variety of activities.

As a Christian school becomes larger, it is not possible to go to every sports event for girls, every sports event for boys, every concert, etc. You are not expected to have perfect attendance. It is possible to support every event that only comes up once or twice a year such as a basketball tournament, a major dramatic production, a retreat, etc.

A few Christian school teachers feel that they are only obligated for school activities which fall during the school day within the daily time limits set by their contracts. Technically that may be true. It is not a matter of being required to attend activities contractually. It would be better to stay at home than to come under duress. If you view the school as the outpouring of your life, giving time for being with students in activities becomes quite natural and is a happy thing, not a chore. This is analogous to a pastor who gives himself to his congregation without being a clockwatcher who is jealous of his own time.

Sponsoring Activities

Teachers are asked frequently to help with activities in addition to their classroom responsibilities. This is part of the Christian school's ministry and should be done gladly and well.

This extra work does not fall to everyone equally even though principals always do their best to equate the total load of teachers. Activities fall heavier on teachers who have greater talents or experience in various areas. To illustrate, a teacher who is not musical will not be asked to help with the school choir. A teacher who is musical will probably be asked to use that ability in a variety of ways. That is Scriptural, for the Bible says that to whom much is given, much is required.

When a school is small there are not many faculty members to go around on activities, and you will be asked to sponsor activities for which you are not completely qualified. Accept this as a challenge, a fresh opportunity to trust God, and do your best. It will be a learning experience professionally and spiritually. As the school grows, relinquish that responsibility when a more qualified person comes on the faculty. Do not hold on to it in a possessive way, for you did your part. God has other things for you now.

Some schools pay extra for sponsoring or coaching, but many do not. The schools who do pay usually pay a token amount, recognition not remuneration. To put it another way, no teacher sponsors or coaches to make money. It is a service above the call of duty. God sees this and He has said that if you give a cup of water in His name it will be remembered in heaven.

Sponsors and coaches experience special blessings. This work opens extraordinary opportunities for deep and lasting relationships with the students. These personal relationships open opportunities to infuence students for God at a level of effectiveness that is the highest in the school. Money cannot equal that pay.

The P.T.F.

Most Christian schools have the equivalent of a P.T.A., though it is most often called by a different name. In the Christian schools it is a fellowship of the parents and the teachers. Therefore, it is referred to as P.T.F. The parent-teacher relationship is one of the chief strengths of the school, and the P.T.F. meetings are expressive of that sincere relationship.

Sensitive teachers understand that they have a ministry to fathers and to mothers through P.T.F. Helping parents to rear their children at home in the nurture and admonition of the Lord is a worthy use of your time. Helping parents understand each of their children is an intimate ministry which most parents appreciate.

The Christian school is most effective in the lives of the students who come from the strongest Christian homes. Anything that strengthens the home will enhance the work of the teacher in the school. A teacher who does not see the school and home complementing each other, but feels that his only responsibility is to the child during school hours, does not comprehend the broad picture of Christian education. Consider your involvement with P.T.F. to be opportune, not an intrusion upon your life.

Faculty Socials

Outside accrediting agencies frequently commend Christian school teachers for being hard workers. While working hard, there is a need for selected social activities among school personnel. There is something about sharing a leisurely meal which knits people together. This is furthered by conversation, by devotions, and by prayer. It helps you to know others.

Faculty-staff socials are normally placed on the master school calendar at the outset of the new school year. It is wise to put them into your personal date book for the year immediately, for the months and weeks fill up rapidly. Plan your personal activities to include each of these special affairs.

A teacher who does not attend a faculty social for other than an emergency is saying that fellowship with his colleagues is not his priority for that evening. A teacher who does this consistently intensifies the fact. If it is not a happy thing for a teacher to attend faculty socials, he should move on to another job where he can enjoy the company of those with whom he works.

District or Regional Christian School Meetings

Teachers are needed as volunteers to help with state or regional Christian school programs. This service will enable you to meet people from other schools. Cooperation in joint efforts for the good of a number of fellow schools develops a deeper sense of cohesion, a deeper sense that you are part of "God's School System". You begin to see things from the broad perspective.

Annual conventions and periodic meetings require programming, planning, and prepared seminar leaders. Take a wide view of the Christian School Movement, think beyond the four walls of your own school, and accept an invitation to serve in any capacity as a blessing from God as He widens your ministry. You will be enriched, blessed. There could be a surprise blessing as you extend yourself to help others. It could be the beginning of a relationship that would last for a long time.

Perspective on Activities

Activities are important in a good school, but they are secondary to the instructional program. Students usually prefer activities to study. Teachers sometimes prefer an activity over a classroom period. This is not bad, if activities are kept in perspective and not permitted to dominate the work.

The Bible says that much study is a weariness to the flesh. When weariness is punctuated by well planned activity, the school day is better. School is work, however, and although you will create a happy classroom, it would not be correct to give your students the impression that school should be only fun. An overemphasis on the place of activities may be a reaction to the mental discipline in the hard work of learning.

There are natural times during the year when activities should have extra time. For example, the choir needs additional practices before the Christmas program or before the spring concert. The drama club must have a dress rehearsal before its production is presented. Do not begrudge students that time by making them feel bad about missing your class that day.

An academic teacher whose overriding interest is in an activity area to the point that he only endures the classroom, will not be effective in instruction. It would be better for that person to switch jobs or to switch schools to get into a situation where that activity area would become his main assignment. That would probably mean a move to a larger school where there is a full-time position in that activity. To illustrate, a social studies teacher whose main interest in education is coaching varsity sports should move into physical education. A fifth grade classroom teacher whose consuming interest is music should move into music education.

In both examples, additional training would be needed. It is worth the effort to get additional training to qualify for a position you like. The alternative, spending your teaching career in a position you do not enjoy very much, is not acceptable. In general, life is long enough to prepare for what you enjoy. This is Biblical, for in Psalm 37 God says, "Delight thyself also in the Lord: and He shall give thee the desires of thine heart."

Always encourage your students to take leadership in activities. Put yourself in the background. Activities are for their development, not a platform for your own star performance.

Activity Groups and the Community

Certain activities lend themselves to presentation in the community. This gives an outreach and develops poise and confidence in the students. It is the equivalent of an important game in athletics.

Scheduling activity groups for outside engagements can become tangled unless the leaders sit down at the outset of the school year with the annual calendar and negotiate in friendly terms for the dates during the year. Since some students are involved in several activities, dates should not be too close together even though they are different activities. Church calendars should also be consulted.

Outside activities by the school must not draw students away from their church involvement. There may be occasional conflicts if the school serves students from many churches. Careful governing is required to keep these conflicts minimal. It is important for the school to encourage students to be totally involved in their local churches. That nerve must never be harmed.

When you take your group out into the community, do not appeal to them to do their best because they are representing the Christian school. Stress the truth that they are representing the Lord. It is their responsibility to please Him, to give their performance heartily as to the Lord. When you and your group please the Lord, He will take care of the reputation of your school. Your approach will not be one of rah-rah the school, but one of directing the attention of people to the Lord of the school.

School Publications and Press Releases

It is not unusual for a teacher to be asked to write something for a school publication or for a press release. Accept that invitation, and use it to sharpen your writing skill. Writing may not be your favorite pastime, but it is a part of your teaching ministry.

As in school activities, direct attention toward God as much as possible in your writing. Do not approach it in the world's attitude of public relations. It bears repeating: if you honor God in your writing, He will take care of the testimony of your school. People's hearts will be moved, and they will make the effort to get more information about the school.

Although writing helps the school to become known in the community, the major thing that causes a Christian school to grow is quality classroom teaching day in and day out. A good brochure or an interesting article will catch attention, but the endorsement of the school by satisfied parents to their friends moves those friends to enroll their own chil-

61

dren. The word gets around when students and parents like the school. Similarly, the word gets around when students and parents do not like the school. No amount of writing will counteract deep displeasure with the school.

Lending a Helping Hand

There are times when we professional educators have to pitch in and lend a helping hand around the school. It seems that there are always times when chairs must be set up or taken down, tables or desks moved, decorations to be made or stored, etc. This is too much for one or two people. Many hands make light work, and you are needed.

Some teachers take to this more than others. They have the spiritual gift of helps recorded in 1 Corinthians 12:28. Because it is more natural for such a person, this does not imply that only people so gifted should be helpers.

If you have a particular trade, you may be in a position to help the school considerably. An electrician, for example, can do many things around a school. So can a professional painter.

Many schools have periodic work days for parents and for older students. If you participate in these days, you will get to know people. That helps in your teaching and in the counseling part of your ministry with both students and parents. Building closer relationships through a work day is a greater outcome than the money saved by doing the jobs yourself. Your involvement is appreciated and noted even though people probably will not mention it to you. It is a practical identification with them on behalf of the school.

Home and Home Visits

Inviting students to your own home for a meal and for a visit is one of the warmest things you can do for them. God uses it impressively, for they remember the visit for years. Perhaps it is the fact that you have been willing to share the privacy of your home with them that makes the experience meaningful. The relaxed conversation, fun, and counsel is part of it, too.

Welcome all students to your home over a period of time. If you only invite a select few, the uninvited will have negative feelings. This is understandable and can be avoided by simple records and open invitations to all. You certainly do not want this good thing to go sour because students think you invite only your pets to your home. Better to invite none than to only invite a few.

Make room in your social calendar to accept invitations to the homes of your students. Students usually enjoy having you in their homes. It is a good experience for them and will give you insights into their family life which will enable you to minister to them more effectively at school.

Some parents and students may begin to invite you to their homes too frequently. When you sense that this is beginning to happen, decline graciously. You must always guard against an abnormally close relationship with any parent or with any student. That can occur, and it is difficult to correct. It is far wiser to keep it from happening in the first place. Be friendly, visit in homes, but keep a professional distance at all times.

Serious Illness or Accidents

Your presence is a blessing and an encouragement when one of your students or parents is seriously ill or hurt. Go to the hospital or to the home when you learn of serious trouble or of death. This includes students and parents from prior years, not just your students of this year.

Sometimes there is a tendency not to do this because you are unsure of what to say. God knows that and He will help you to do the right thing when you get there. Commit the visit to Him in prayer and go ahead. If you find deep grief when you arrive, you may not say anything, but will simply weep with those who weep. The gift of your presence is what ministers to the people, for they know that you love them.

Handling Student Money

Extreme care should be exercised in handling student money lest there be the slightest suspicion of wrongdoing. Take the time to record everything at the time the money comes under your care. Take the cash and checks to the school office and get a receipt immediately. Do not leave the money in your desk or in your purse or pocket. Do not carry it around with you. Never take it home.

If you are responsible for a student who is a treasurer for an activity or an organization, supervise him. Write clear guidelines for handling the money and require everything to be done by the guidelines. There is no room for improvising in handling money at school. Some students have gotten into wrongdoing with school money because they were not adequately supervised by a teacher, and the temptation was great.

Long Range Activity Planning

When a Christian school is young or when it is small, much work is needed to develop good activities of high caliber. This maturing is best accomplished by careful long-range planning. Lay out a five-year plan for the progress of your activity. Note the number of students to be recruited each year, the scheduling to be done, the space to be obtained, the personnel to be added, and the money to be budgeted.

Visualize the five-year plan as a cylinder rotating toward you. As this year passes, add a new fifth year at the end of your plan and revise the other four years as warranted. This way you always have a five-year plan, as contrasted to completing the entire five years before establishing a new five-year plan.

This year's plans are bound to be more accurate than the plans for the fourth or fifth years. Validity will increase with experience, and you will even surprise yourself at times with the accuracy of your projections. This work is highly creative, and you will like it.

Student Fund Raising Activities

Each Christian school establishes its own standards for student fund raising. Find out those standards and be sure to follow them. If you learn that standards and procedures have not been spelled out, talk to the principal and get administrative approval before you begin a fund-raising activity. This is a sensitive area in the Christian school, and you should not do what you think is right in your own eyes, for you can get yourself out on a limb without realizing it.

Get involved with approved activities. This is a good way to give of yourself to the students. They like it when a teacher participates with them in a car wash, a walkathon, a bake sale, etc. They open up to you when you take time to do these things with them. Never approach this an an encroachment upon your time, for students are perceptive and can tell your heart is not in it.

Encouraging Students in Activities

Some students need encouragement to try out for activities. A word from you can stimulate them to it. If they are successful, participation in the activity can build their ego and be a wholesome influence upon their personality.

You will have a feel for the child's capacity to be successful in a given activity and should steer him into the right ones. If he is unsuccessful, come up with a viable alternative which he can handle. Do not leave him down or dangling.

Encouraging Parent Support of Activities

There are times when a parent does not comprehend the importance of supporting his child in school activities. You can help by talking to the parent about it. Explain the purpose of the activity, and show the values of parental support to the child.

Other times you will have to temper parents who are over-zealous in supporting their children. They need counsel to keep things in balance. The pressures they put upon their children are unreasonable, and they need you to point this out to them. This happens more frequently in athletics than in other activities.

Behaviour at Athletic Events

A good athletic program for girls and boys builds school morale more than any other thing. Winning teams excite the entire school and create strong feelings of loyalty. You should be part of this scene even though you cannot attend each game, as some of the parents do.

Part of your Christian testimony before your students is your behaviour at games as a spectator or as a coach. People do not talk to you about this, but they watch you. The major test comes when there is heavy pressure and adversity, when things are not going well for your team. If you yell at the refs, razz the opponents, lose your temper, etc., do not expect your class to respect you as a Christian, or listen intently when you teach in Bible class or speak in chapel. Your game behaviour will override your message.

Students follow the example of teachers, and especially of coaches, at ball games. The actions of the crowd usually reflect the actions of the coach. A controlled coach can quiet an upset crowd, but an intemperate coach cannot. Remember, you are living before God at a ball game as well as in the classroom. You can please Him at a game, or you can displease Him. It is not worth it to lose your testimony over a game.

Chaperoning Activities

It takes additional work by teachers to keep an activities program moving smoothly. Although you may not be the sponsor, you will probably be asked to chaperone for a concert, a game, a play, or a class trip. This is a serious thing, for it takes all of your attention for a sustained period to be a good chaperone who is alert to what is happening, who is supervising to keep untoward things from happening. Do not leave the students unattended while you talk to the other chaperones.

Chaperoning often involves extra transportation help in getting children around. You will be amazed at the casual attitude of some parents in not planning all of the transportation for their children. Accept this graciously, and have a good talk with the students while you are driving them around.

Some schools have been hurt deeply by incidents which happened at school activities because the chaperones were not doing their job. It is a mistake to think that Christian students from Christian schools do not need close chaperoning. The devil is active against our students, and he does not ease off during activities.

Social Needs of Students

A student's attitude toward school is influenced strongly by his social acceptance. Wise teachers observe the social life of their students all day, and work quietly to keep anyone from being on the outside of the group.

Jesus was so good at this. He emphasized the worth of the individual, even though each had sinned. He pointed out the need for wholesome relationships between persons. He showed the way to the greatest of all relationships, that of men to God. The gospels speak of all these things, and are superior to any other psychological approach.

Spiritual training is always primary in the school. Look upon social training as part of spiritual training, for it is, and its importance will be evident. You are developing persons through your teaching, not just transmitting subject matter.

It is sad when students leave the Christian school because

they feel the class is dominated by a few cliques, and they are unaccepted. A Christian education is lost because social needs were not met. Students who drop out for social reasons rarely return in subsequent years. They seldom reveal that this is the reason for leaving. When they do, it is frequently too late to bring about healing to rectify the situation.

Encouraging Church Activities

The Christian school works harmoniously with the home and with the evangelical church. Some view this as a tripod, some as a triangle. Others see it as a three-fold cord, which is not easily broken.

The point is: The school is supportive of the church. Our students must be encouraged to look to the church for spiritual development without allowing their spiritual activities at the school to replace their involvement at church. The school is to supplement, not to supplant.

This is not an easy thing, and you will have to pay attention to it. Often the spiritual activities of the school are on a better level than those of some churches. You can see how students can easily begin to look to the school at the expense of looking away from their home church. That is a compliment to the school. It is also a mistake. Christian school students should be among the leaders in their local churches and should work to have a good program.

A serious problem arises especially at the high school level when Christian school students are not encouraged to participate in the activities of their church. If they are turned off to church, it is conceivable that they will still be turned on to the spiritual emphasis of the school, because the school's spiritual programs are lively. The problem emerges following graduation from the school. The graduate no longer looks to the school for spiritual growth, and he has not looked to his church for several years. It is a dilemma. Some graduates do not look to God to get out of this dilemma, and languish in spiritual deserts for years suffering from the drought of no fellowship in church with God's people. They go against the biblical admonition to not forsake the assembling of ourselves together. If you are ministering at the high school level, do not be a contributor to that problem; but keep your students away from a collision course with it by being active and positive in their churches.

Chapter Four

UNDERSTANDING ADMINISTRATION, POLICIES, AND PROCEDURES

Each Christian school has the freedom to set its organizational structure, its policies, and its procedures. All of this is important, for it is the framework within which you are teaching. Do not take the position that you are an academic teacher to whom these matters are insignificant. They affect you each day and are vital.

Policies and procedures, even the administrative structure, are open to revision as the school grows and matures. Because they are changeable, they should never be considered on a par with God's Word, which is unchanging and settled forever in heaven. To elaborate, a school needs organization, policies, and procedures to reach its objectives, its reason for existence. The school has the right to establish these items according to what is believed to be God's leading for that individual school. Yet, these should not be viewed as statements saying, "Thus saith the Lord." They are man-made, and it is all right to modify them as warranted. That is not comparable to tampering with the fundamental doctrines of Christianity, which must be guarded against with all diligence in the Christian school.

Understanding
The Organizational Structure

Ask the principal for your own copy of the school's organizational chart. This will show the position of the school board, the principal, other administrators, the faculty, the staff and the church, or the parent body. Notice three things in particular: First, note the job or committee titles; second, note the lines of authority which delineate accountability within the organization; and third, note who stands in an advisory capacity to whom.

Raise questions with the principal until you understand the positions in the school, the direct accountability functioning in the school, and the advisory relationships which exist. Be certain to comprehend your position within the organizational structure. In particular, learn to whom you are accountable for your performance. Define those whose relationship to you is advisory rather than a relationship of direct authority over you. Knowing the organizational structure of the school and fulfilling your role within its pattern will deliver you from the serious problems and misunderstandings that would crop up if you went your own way and did what was right in your own eyes.

If the principal does not have a copy of the school's organizational chart to give you, ask him to take a few minutes and sketch it out for you on paper. It is that important a matter for you, and he will be glad to do that. If you find that he does not have the understanding to do this for you, be wary and cautious in those areas where he is fuzzy. If he does not comprehend certain areas, it seems reasonable to conclude that he will not be able to back you if you do something not quite right in someone else's eyes in those wobbly areas. Tell him that you would appreciate his review of the matter, and request that he follow through by giving you a copy of the organizational structure within a time limit which is fair to him.

Following the Chain of Command

Authority is of God and creates the climate within which the school can function happily and achieve its goals. Those in authority are not better persons than you. God says that leaders are to be respected for their work's sake. Since the school is Christian, they are over you in the Lord, and God says that we are to obey those who are over us in Him. (Hebrews 13:17).

Occasionally teachers misunderstand Christian school administration and feel that everyone should have an equal say in the operation of the school. The Christian school is not a teacher-run school. Good administrators value the opinions of teachers and do not act like lords over God's heritage, but the principal is the chief administrative officer of the school and bears the final responsibility for the school's daily and yearly operations.

The chain of command within the school is not intended to squelch your creativity or to stifle your voice. The Scriptures also say that God's people should be subject to one another regardless of who holds the position of authority. Experienced Christian school administrators thank God for His guidance to them through individual teachers and staff members, and through faculty committees. Say what you think.

Because of his position, the principal must sometimes make decisions which are unpopular. When that happens do not cause dissension by murmuring against him when he did not do what you wished. Realize that you are in an advisory position to him. That is an important role which you fulfill, but he must make the decision as he sees it before the Lord, and sometimes he will not follow your advice. Do not pout or withdraw from him because he did not follow your counsel that time. Perhaps this is a little like the relationship between the President and his cabinet. There are times when his decision is not the consensus of the group.

When the teachers and administrators are functioning well

by understanding their roles and by applying Christian body-life principles in their daily relationships, the administration of the school is wondrous, a beautiful thing, an evidence of God's leadership and control of the school. Each teacher is fulfilled, each administrator is fulfilled, and the ministry moves forward because the Holy Spirit has freedom. If the Spirit is grieved, these things will not be true and the ministry is hindered. Take care that you are never the cause of hindrance in the school where you are serving God.

Respect for the School Board

The board of the school has a strong influence on you and your work through the policies which they establish and through their major decisions. You probably will not see them on campus very often, but be sensitive to their importance in the life of the school. Respect them and their work.

In general, American education is moving toward an adversary position between the school board and teachers. This must not be the practice, or the spirit, in the Christian school. The relationship must be harmonious, not disjointed.

Talk to board members and get to know them. Do not discuss with them the things which you should take to the principal. Understand that the board is not responsible for the daily administration of the school. The board establishes policies and the principal is the daily administrator functioning within those policies. It is serious to by-pass the principal by talking to a board member about administrative matters. That is unprofessional, a breach of ethics.

It is possible for you to have an influence upon the board. Your major influence can be through prayer for them. God says that the prayers of a righteous person have a powerful effect. It is not simple to fulfill the responsibilities of the board, for they are called upon to make heavy decisions. They must be adept at discerning God's will, for frequently they must make decisions when all of the relevant information is unavailable. They must be persons of strong faith, willing to move the school in the direction in which God leads.

There may be times in the life of a Christian school when the principal or the school board are unduly attacked. Pray that this will not happen in your school. If it does, stand quietly but firmly in their defense. True, God stands with them, but they will be disheartened if all men leave them. The devil, that roaring lion, seeks to devour schools in this way, and he must be resisted by looking to God and by standing with those who are maligned.

The Faculty Handbook

It is rare to find a faculty handbook that reads like a literary classic. While you are at the school the handbook will be a classic to you, to be read, and re-read. It gives you the guidelines within which to exercise your creative talents. Mark up your copy, digest it.

The handbook gives you boundaries. As long as you are within the boundaries the principal can back you. If you go out of bounds, willfully or ignorantly, the principal cannot back you. That is a precarious position, undesirable. Do not improvise. Go by the book.

There may be a few things in the handbook with which you disagree. Follow the channels in the school for possible revision. Until revision, follow the handbook for it is the authority. You cannot be selective and say that you only accept part of it.

The Bible and the handbook are not equal. The Bible is first, by far. It is wrong, though, to despise the handbook by treating it lightly. That attitude can hurt you, sometimes badly.

Enforcing School Policies

Part of your ministry is enforcing school policies and procedures, including those which you may not like. Until they

are changed you must go along with them. Serious break-
downs occur when you, or several teachers, do not fulfill
your responsibilities in this area. It pressurizes the teachers
who are enforcing the policies and puts them in an unfair
position. Students like teachers who do not enforce unpopular policies and use the example of those teachers as leverage
against the teachers who are doing right. When that occurs,
the right teacher is made to look bad. That inversion should
not and cannot be tolerated in the school. Calling right
wrong and wrong right is warned against in the Scriptures.

The attitude of the teacher while explaining and enforcing
school policies is contagious and is picked up quickly by his
students. If you have a wholesome approach, your students
will go along well. If you have a negative approach, your
class will be negative. No homeroom or class lives to itself.
Everything you do affects the school, affects the entire body.
Never visualize yourself as influencing only the students directly in your class. You touch many beyond them, through
them.

Keep up-to-date with changes in school policies. Mark the
revision in your faculty handbook with the effective date.
You do not want to put yourself in the awkward position of
enforcing an old policy that has been superceded. That
makes you appear to be out of it, and no teacher wants that
taint upon his reputation. We teachers are expected to be
with it.

Faculty Dress Code

If your Christian school has a faculty dress code you have
company, for most schools do. Live well within the boundaries of that code rather than seeing how close you can dress
to the line without stepping over the mark. Students observe
the attitudes of their teachers toward dress codes. Be gentle,
not irked.

Consider this: Wearing certain clothing and adhering to
certain standards of grooming is a small price to pay in order

to serve God in a Christian school. Do not allow the faculty dress code to be a stumbling block to you. Do not let it deter you from your ministry. Give up some of your liberty willingly, for in that you are becoming all things to all men that you might win some, as the apostle Paul said.

Usually the dress code is up for administrative review every year. Express your feelings to the proper persons at that time. Do not foment unrest all year about the code. That underground fire sometimes becomes a seething issue which can harm the school. It is sad to see a Christian school reeling under uncontrolled dissent about dress codes. Somtimes a school almost eats itself up over this issue. It takes a school years to recover and regain its poise and composure after people's teeth have been set on edge over dress.

This does not imply that your school is wrong if it has a faculty or a student dress code. The point is, live peaceably within the code until it is revised, if ever. A chafing Christian school teacher may think that he is covering his attitude, but that is impossible. He is the one who is deceived, not his children or his colleagues.

Criticism

It is probable that there will always be a few things at the school which you do not like too much. Apart from purity of doctrine, everyone at the school has to give in a little on what he thinks is best for the school to function. Be tolerant in those areas where you disagree somewhat and do not let them grow into major issues with you. It is childish to be petulant about these things and to bicker because they have not gone your way. Use the proper channels for voicing disagreement, do it graciously, and rest those matters with the Lord. He has ways of turning things around.

Criticism, complaining, in the presence of students is especially damaging. What you think has been spoken in confidence will probably spread to others. This is the biblical principle which states that things spoken in your bedchamber will be taken by a bird and broadcast to those outside. Students are quick and pick up critical words by a teacher. Even if they do not repeat them, they should not have to hear them and carry them in their minds and hearts. They will not know it if you rescind your criticism and will think that your words still hold.

Discussing Students
With Other Parents

Sometimes a parent will begin to discuss a child who is not his own with you. It is a matter of professional ethics not to do this. What you know about the other children is a special trust of information to be used in working with them and their parents alone. It is information to be shared with teachers and administrators to help them minister to the children, but it is not for others. This is a danger in a Christian school for there is such an open spirit.

There is wisdom in using another teacher for a confidant rather than a homeroom mother or another parent. Some parents have a warm, personable way about them and are easy to talk to. Some can draw confidential information from you without your realizing it. This can come under a spiritual umbrella for the parent may ask for details in order to pray intelligently about you, your class, and the school. Continue to be professional in this matter at all times for it is nothing to God to save by many or by few. People do not have to know everything for God to act on behalf of the children or others.

Answering Common Questions

When people learn that you are teaching in the Christian school they will ask you questions about your job and about the school. Be ready to answer those questions. You are part of the public relations program of the school and should be able to speak intelligently about it. When you do not know an answer, make a note of the question and do your best to get back to the person. If you cannot, at least you will know the answer if that question is raised again.

Among questions raised most frequently are the following: Is the school accredited? How much is tuition? Are the teachers certified? What is the sports program? Is there a band or an orchestra? Does the school have a choir? What are the requirements for admission? How does a teacher apply for a job at the school? Who is the principal and what are his qualifications? How many of the teachers hold master's degrees? What is the enrollment? How many students are in a class? How do incoming transfer students fare? What is the annual budget? Is there a pay scale for teachers? Are there fringe benefits for faculty and staff? How many board members are there? How does transportation work? Do students buy their books? Is there a hot lunch program? What percentage of the students are girls? Are elementary classes self-contained? What are the electives in the high school? How is high school morale? Are the students well-disciplined? Is the school traditional or progressive? Are there open classrooms? Does the school allow visitors? Is the school integrated? What is the attitude of the students toward spiritual things? What percentage of the students have accepted Christ? What churches do the teachers belong to? Are student leaders Christians? Does the school ever expel students? What are the policies on tuition payments? In what state, regional, and national organizations does the school hold membership? Is there a dress code? What are parents required to do beyond paying tuition? How does the school raise money? Are parents used as volunteer aides? How old is the school? What percentage of the high school graduates go to Christian colleges? What percentage of the high school graduates go into Christian work? Does the school accept state or federal aid? What are the long range plans for the future?

No list like this can be exhaustive. People will ask you new and unexpected things. That is stimulating and you will handle it well, for it is fun to talk about your ministry.

Be candid for every school has its shortcomings. People

accept honest answers, but you will be suspect if you try to pull the wool over their eyes by trying to make the school look better than it is. There is always more that the school can do, always room to improve what it is doing. It is an evidence of maturity, not of weakness, to evaluate the school honestly.

Since the philosophy of Christian education is correct, encourage questioners to stand with the school in improving its facilities and program. The school may not be what it should be, but it needs the help of many people to become what it should be. The approach of sitting on the sidelines to see whether or not the school is going to fly misses the point that the school is philosophically correct and must fly. Challenge people who are waiting to jump on the band wagon after things get moving to put their shoulder to the wheel right now and help to further this testimony to Jesus Christ in the educational world.

Direct Dealing With The Principal

Psychological studies indicate that the most significant factor in a person's attitude toward his job is his feeling about his immediate superior. Many would say that salary is the biggest factor, but it is not. When the spiritual dimension of our work in the Christian school is added to this, the importance of the teacher-principal relationship is apparent.

Foster this relationship by being friendly, open, and direct with your principal. View him as a co-worker, not as an adversary. Seek opportunities on a regular basis and informally to speak to him. Avoid any tendency to shy away from him. He needs you.

Principals, like teachers, are busy people and are sometimes hard to see. If he is unavailable and the matter you want to discuss with him has a time value, write a note and leave it in an obvious spot on his desk. Tell his secretary about the note and tell her when you will stop back for an answer.

The secretary to the principal can be helpful in keeping you in touch with the principal. She knows his schedule. Frequently she knows what he has said or what his thinking is on a matter, and is able to answer your question or give you an idea of what he may say. Although her answer is unofficial, there are times when it is beneficial to find out the direction in which the principal is thinking. Recognize that this is tentative, for administrators are well-known for sometimes changing direction without explaining everything to their secretaries.

Sometimes a teacher will carry note writing too far. The principal wants to work with you directly not by correspondence. Interface is necessary to cultivate a strong professional relationship between you.

The Contract

Psalm 15 says that the godly man swears to his own hurt and does not change. Keep your contract once you have signed it. Sometimes a teacher will break a contract saying that God is leading him to do that. The Bible does not support that position.

Since the contract is binding, you must believe that it is God's will before you sign it. Solomon writes in Ecclesiastes that it is better not to vow a thing than to vow and fail to fulfill it. If you are not certain about signing the contract, it is reasonable to conclude that this is not God's will and you should not enter the agreement. The Bible says that when we know God's will it is attended by the peace of God in our hearts, which is in contrast to uncertainty. The peace of God is your umpire in the decision. This is practical, a gift from God.

The Biblical parable of the workers in the vineyard who received the same pay whether they worked the whole day or half a day teaches that it is wrong to complain about wages once they have been agreed upon. That is not an easy parable for the employer was not equitable in his dealings. That emphasizes the point, which is clear: It is wrong to gripe about salary after you have accepted the terms. To quibble at that time is wrong.

Leaving the School

Returning to the school next year should never be a mechanical decision. Each year you need the assurance that God wants you to serve Him here next year. That is as true for your twenty-fifth year as it was for your first year. This leading of God in your life must always be fresh.

God may lead you to make a change. The deepest indication of this will be a restlessness in your spirit. This may be related to something which has happened at school. It may not. When you sense that the cloud is starting to lift and it is time for you to move, you must follow that leading. He has something new for you. Accept it, for His will is characterized by three key words; good, acceptable and perfect.

If you are leaving because of dissatisfaction, keep your own counsel. Do not cut up people and the school on your way out. Outbursts at public meetings, open letters to the school family, or publishing your letter of resignation to the board, etc. do not accomplish God's work. They wound and they hurt, often for years. Such a leaving will not improve your recommendation for your next position. Word of the manner of your departure will follow you. If you did it graciously, your reputation will be enhanced. If you did it bitterly, people will be wary lest you do the same thing after a few years in your new school. Do not tear down any of the work you accomplished while at the school by leaving in the wrong way.

It is wise not to resign unless you mean it. Occasionally a teacher will use resignation like a trial balloon to get a reading on how the people at the school feel about him. If people beg him to stay, he withdraws his resignation giving the impression that the school is lucky to get him back next year. That practice is not good. You are in God's service and He is the One who commands you. A play for recognition is a sure sign of an insecure teacher.

Scheduling Field Trips
and Activities

Field trips and activities add zest to the program of the school. They can be overdone, but the tendency for some teachers is to avoid them because of the added responsibility and work. Seeing the way God uses these in the growth of the children makes it worth every telephone call, every problem, every expense, every aching foot.

Children get excited about field trips and any cancellation or postponement disappoints them. To avoid that, get administrative approval for the activity well in advance. Secondly, be certain that the date is open on the master calendar of the school. When those two things are in order, record your event on the calendar so other teachers will see that the date is taken and will not schedule conflicting events. The record on the calendar is official in case of a dispute.

There is more responsibility upon you whenever you take a class off campus. Parents or other teachers may serve as aides or chaperones, but you have the final responsibility and the top authority to see that things are done according to your approval. Recognize your position and carry things through to meet your objectives. Do not allow an agressive parent or fellow teacher to usurp your position.

Ordering Books and Supplies

The faculty handbook will spell out the procedures for ordering the things that you need. In general, place your order on the form requesting purchase and submit it to the principal for approval. He will approve it, ask for clarification, or disapprove it. Be ready to justify the expense. Sometimes it is good to attach a paragraph of justification to the request. Upon approval your order is transferred to an official school purchase order and sent to the vendor. It always seems to take more time than you think to get delivery, so place your order in good time. There may be times of temporary financial pinch when only emergency items may be ordered. A good school cannot be run like that for very long. Everything will not come to you in one year, but you must make good progress each year and build up quickly to have everything you need for excellence in your work.

Chapter Five

PRACTICAL
PERSONAL ITEMS

What the teacher is as a person determines his effectiveness as a Christian school teacher. His values, his doctrinal beliefs, his commitment, his attitudes all come out over a period of time in the classroom. There is no neutral teacher.

Teaching in the school is living with the students, with the faculty and staff, and to a small degree, with parents. This means giving yourself to others, with all of the give and take of daily school life. The relationships are close. That is good, but it means you cannot live unto yourself.

Some practical personal items are presented in this section. Each is not equally important, but none is unimportant. Considered together, the cumulative effect will become apparent. Some summarize previous thoughts.

Commitment to Excellence

It is not enough for the school to be good, or even accredited. We represent Christ in the educational world and our greatest desire is to see Him receive honor through the school. We want the school to be approved unto God, the commendation which is superior to any recognition by the world.

Most Christian school teachers perform well enough to keep their jobs. Some work harder than others. It is not a matter of keeping your job or working hard when you talk about a commitment to excellence. That commitment speaks of the characteristics of teachers who would be in the top ten percent as professional educators. It speaks of motivation to serve Christ ably. It speaks of being wholehearted in the ministry of the school.

Be responsive to God's dealings with you. Ask Him to deepen your dedication to Him and to your ministry. Pursue excellence, avoid mediocrity. This will require a million personal sacrifices. It does not come cheaply.

Handling Pressure

Christian school teaching is not an easy job. There are many pressures, some of them intense. Other pressures from our personal lives are always with us, fluctuating in seriousness. Our trust in God must be a lively, growing thing to cope with life. The Word tells us to count it all joy when life presses upon us and look to God for wisdom and strength. As teachers we do not deny pressures. We see them realistically, but believe that God is with us in them. Nothing is beyond the scope of His control in our school life or in our life out of school. Nothing.

There are days when you will step into your classroom with a heavy heart, under extreme pressure. You will not be able to explain to your students. God will give you special strength and you will experience Him deeply. Your teaching will reflect a closer walk with God.

On those days be careful about making major decisions. Try to delay them so they will not be made under strong duress. Do not do anything precipitously. Trust God and wait. He uses time as a great healer. The tincture of time is good medicine for we begin to see things from His viewpoint.

Try not to lose your composure before the class on pressure days. The scene of a teacher losing his temper or crying before the class is not good. Knowing that you are under pressure, be careful not to overreact to the normal irritations of the classroom. Little things can seem big. Be especially careful of what you say. Be a bit quieter and subdued that day.

Wait quietly upon God for the renewal of strength He promises. After the pressures pass, you will look back upon those days and quietly thank God for Jesus, who never leaves us or forsakes us. In years to come you will be able to minister to others as they come under the pressures you have experienced. Your counsel will be wise for you have been under the same things and have seen God and His Word applied in the situation. You will see that there was Divine purpose in your suffering. God is developing your shepherd's heart.

Courage With Parents

Christian school teachers are partners with the parents in the education of the students. This partnership is strong. Since it is close, you will get to know students and their parents well. You will note strengths and weaknesses. Over a period of a school year you will get a good focus on the child and his parents.

There are times when you must talk to parents about problems their children are having. The parents may be aware of the matter, but not always. All parents suffer from a degree of halo effect in looking at their own children. Sometimes you are the one to break hard news to them. You may need administrative support in this, so do not hesitate to involve the principal. It is part of his job to help you in these situations.

Some parents will thank you for pointing these things out. Others will react negatively to you. Always be kind, courteous and professional.

Accept Reproof

One of the proofs that we have been born again is the chastening of God in our lives. Hebrews 12 says that if we do not experience that we are not sons of God. The book of Proverbs says that reproofs of instruction are the way of life. Further, the person who refuses reproof errs.

Do not let the authority you have as a teacher blind you to the fact that you have a lot to learn. A know-it-all attitude is not becoming to a teacher. We teachers are also students in God's school of life. We must not be hardhearted or stiff-necked, but soft and open so that God can guide us with His eye. As we get graduate degrees and added years of experience, we must still accept reproof from the Bible or from people. We will not get beyond that in this life. That graduation will occur when we are promoted to glory. The teacher who remains teachable is the one who reaches his potential.

Punctuality

Sometimes you feel that you have been going to school all of your life and your life is controlled by school bells. Summer vacations are refreshing because you can get off the clock for a change. It is true that we live by the clock in our work.

The nature of our work demands punctuality. There are no tricks to always being on time. Simply anticipate what is happening and give enough time to get there about five minutes early. In the morning do not count on every traffic light being green in order to be on time.

Do not excuse yourself for tardiness by thinking that you are just naturally slow. If that is the case, you are one who must allow more time to get to everything on time. Do not make the administrator call you to task for tardiness. If it does not seem to bother him you are still wrong, and so is he for not correcting you.

Requesting Help

Principals expect teachers to be able to resolve their own problems instead of referring every little thing to the administrator. Teachers are usually independent people who possess self-confidence. With these two things in mind, it is easy to see why most teachers are hesitant to admit that they need help. That reluctance must be overcome for it can lead to grave trouble.

Administrative personnel and your faculty colleagues are there when you need them. You are part of that body and if you are hurting they need to know it so they can minister to you. Take a few deep breaths, pray, and tell them what is wrong.

Vagaries cloud a request for help. Define the problem clearly, give illustrations of the problem, and list the solutions which you have tried. Give probable reasons for the continuation of the matter. Discuss the spiritual issues and implications. Ask God to give wisdom to the person whose help you are seeking.

Sift through the counsel which you receive and put into action those ideas which you believe are of God. After a reasonable length of time, go back to the person who counseled you and discuss the status of the matter. Thank him, ask additional counsel, or seek out someone else. Always be looking to God for His good hand upon the thing. He is the best problem solver.

No Racial Prejudice

The Christian school falls within the command of Jesus Christ to his disciples that they should teach all nations. This Great Commission is recorded at the end of Matthew 28. Since all nations refers to all races of the world, any taint of racial prejudice in the school is not biblical, but is a perversion of Christ's desire and order. The Christian school is not a segregation academy. It does not exist to avoid integration in education.

To see students and teachers of varied racial heritage working harmoniously in the school is an example of the functioning of the body of Christ. It is universal, made up of all races. The message of Christ's love is for the entire world not for a particular race. The Christian school shows race relations at their best, demonstrating that God enables children, young people, parents, and teachers to work well together with acceptance and concern for each other.

Sound Judgment

Teachers are supposed to have good judgment which is evidenced by making the right decision in something requiring evaluation and response. Good teachers improve their judgment over the years by learning from their experiences. They remember what was right and they remember what was wrong, taking care not to do that again.

Experience is acknowledged to be a good teacher, but it is a limited teacher wherever God is omitted. The better teacher for learning sound judgment is the Bible for it enables us to judge things from God's standpoint. A teacher's judgment of a matter can be right from the world's judgment, but wrong from God's judgment. The Christian School teacher seeks God's sound judgment as revealed in all of Scripture.

The book of Proverbs is pertinent to teachers. As a book of instruction, much of it relates to judgment and practical things that are always coming up in the classroom. There are 31 chapters in the book, which makes it a very nice monthly calendar. Read a chapter a day, go through the book several times and then occasionally, and your judgment in the classroom will grow and sharpen. We are all more worldly minded than we realize and need to be oriented to God's thoughts and to God's ways. Our minds veer away from His thinking so readily.

Talking Too Much

Few Christian school teachers are introverts. Most are good communicators. Most have good vocabularies, active minds, and quick wits. A sharp tongue may also come in that package. Perhaps not.

There are many times when you will be thinking certain things, seeing things, and hearing things that you should not talk about. You do not have to say everything you are thinking. Reserve in speech, apart from speaking while teaching, is a good thing. It is commended in the New Testament as an evidence of spiritual maturity. Its opposite, talking too much, is warned about in the Old Testament saying that the danger of sinning increases as our talking increases.

Housekeeping Responsibilities

This may be hard to accept, but teaching and housekeeping go together in your ministry as a professional. Like it or not the housekeeping has to be done. Make the best of it by always leaving your room in good order at the end of the period or at the end of the day. If you wonder how well you are doing ask the janitor. He can tell you what should be done better.

Students should be taught to do the actual work. You may have to do a little bit, but your job is to organize the work to be done and supervise to see that things are finished. Unless you have been a school janitor, you have no idea how nice it is to clean certain rooms after school, and how hard it is to clean other untidy rooms.

Instill a thankful spirit in your students for the building and campus which God has provided for them. Encourage them to take good care of it, to be proud of its appearance. The school is for them. It is good for morale to have neat rooms and a clean campus.

Care of Equipment and Furniture

The cost of equipment and furniture goes up each year. It is part of your stewardship to see that these things are handled properly. Normal wear is expected. Abuse is to be avoided.

Teachers who really care about quality furniture and equipment find ways to encourage students to take good care of things. To illustrate, it is interesting to note that the desks in one teacher's room get marked up, while the desks in another teacher's room are unmarked. It is good common sense to stay on top of things to see that they are handled well.

Some schools have a policy that students who cause damage or abuse furniture or equipment must pay a fine or possibly replace that item. If your school does this, enforce that policy. When you are called upon to make the assessment on the abuse be heavy not lenient, because things probably cost more than you think. In some cases you must also figure in the salary of the janitor if he is involved. A broken window is an example. The cost of the janitor's time in replacing it must be added to the cost of the glass and the glazing.

Circumstantial Leading

When circumstances appear to be pointing clearly to a given decision, there is a clear need to pray. Circumstances may be showing God's will, but not necessarily. To go by them without praying can have dire consequences.

The classic example of this problem is the account of Joshua and the Gibeonites. God told the Israelites not to make any covenants with other people as they moved into the Promised Land. The Gibeonites were fearful and developed a wise, though devious plan. They came to Joshua and the people wearing old clothes, old shoes, with old wine skins, and moldy bread. They asserted that all of those things were in good shape when they left home. The bread, they said, was hot out of the oven.

The circumstances were visible to Joshua and his men and they made a league with them. Joshua 9:14 says that this was done without seeking counsel at the mouth of the Lord. They did not pray. Later they found that the Gibeonites had lied to them.

Joshua and his men were taken in, but God made them stick to their covenant. There is a big lesson in this: when we make honest mistakes through not praying about a matter, God does not change the consequences. Doubtless, God would have revealed the charade to Joshua if he had prayed. We must always seek counsel of the Lord, even when things look all right.

Flexibility

There are times during the school year when everything does not go according to the scheduling you have planned. Accept those interruptions, those changes, without becoming tense. Do not be so rigid that you cannot bend when that is necessary. You can be a firm teacher and a flexible teacher at the same time.

Things should be well ordered and carefully planned in your class. Flexibility is not the same as being unprepared, taking everything as it comes up, easing along. Sometimes teachers who are very well ordered are most inflexible. They have trouble adjusting to unexpected changes. If you know you are like that, relax and take a longer term view of the school year. A few disruptions here and there will not hurt your class much over the long haul. It is not worth it to get upset.

If the disruptions in daily routine occur frequently, speak to the proper people to correct matters. Being a flexible person does not mean that you accept every little change as being right. Too many changes indicate a need to tighten up. Better organization and good supervision will minimize changes, which is best.

This is a stimulating part of our ministry, for some days we have to be flexible, and some days we have to tighten up. Not only does this keep you on your toes, it keeps you on your knees. God will help you to be sensitive. Your principal will also give you cues.

Attitude Toward Staff Members

Comprehending the idea of the faculty and staff as a body is basic to our ministry for it shows the importance of each person. One member cannot look down on another. Each plays his part and each is needed. This is contrary to the world's view. The world views administrative personnel as first, instructional personnel as second, and non-instructional personnel as third. Attitudes like that are not correct for the Christian school. Any notions of caste must be dealt with in our hearts and in our minds. The chain of command, which is necessary for sound daily operations, should never be interpreted in the sense that some people are better than others. There are not ranks of personnel like that.

The importance of each staff member is easy to illustrate. When a water pipe breaks at D.C. an immediate call goes out for Ivan and Joe. Those two maintenance men, Ivan Akers and Joe Hoekstra, can fix almost anything with bubble gum and a rubber band. In this emergency they are far more important than any administrator or teacher.

At least one Christian school includes every teacher from grades K-12 and every staff member in the processional and recessional of senior commencement. They are all seated in a position of honor during the ceremony. In this way the school is recognizing the unity of the faculty and staff. The school is also thanking each in this public way for his ministry in bringing the seniors to the place of graduation. That procedure is unifying and that recognition is proper, for it is deserved. It is within the biblical injunction to give honor to whom it is due.

A Procrustean Attitude

Good Christian school teachers do not take a procrustean attitude toward students, parents, teachers, or administrators. They realize that people change and do not pigeon-hole them indefinitely into categories according to something they did or according to what they were like. It disheartens students when their teachers mark them a certain way and do not recognize the changes that are happening. God is at work in the school and you must see Him changing people, including yourself.

Continued Interest
In Former Students

It is fun to see your students grow up, and to realize that you had a significant role in their education. Your prime responsibility is your present class, but you can still exert a positive spiritual impact upon your former students. This is through intercessory prayer, a practical and effectual part of your ministry.

A good pattern in this is the biblical figure, Epaphras. Paul told the Colossians that although Epaphras was not with them, he always labored fervently for them in prayers, that they would stand perfect and complete in all the will of God. He did this with great zeal.

Teachers who support their former students in prayer over the years will be rewarded at the Judgment Seat of Christ. Yet, this is not an easy part of your ministry. It must be done as to the Lord because it is carried out in your secret place without recognition. It requires the sustained travail of your soul of which Paul wrote to the Galatians. He said that he travailed in birth again until Christ be formed in them. They were Christians, but were not mature. Accompanying the travail is blessing from God.

Loyalty

Perceive the school as a living institution not as buildings and grounds. The school is people, living, working, praying, sacrificing, so the students can have an academic education which is integrated with the Word of God. This is a great endeavour. It is a wondrous thing. No Christian school is small, no matter what its enrollment, for God is not small.

Be loyal to your school. It has its problems and it probably has its crisis periods, but it is of God. If you cannot be loyal to it make a change. A year of your life at a school is a great investment of your time, and there is no use to stay at a school when you have a disloyal heart. That is not good for you or for the school. Sometimes a teacher is loyal, but his loyalty shifts as he becomes more interested in things outside of the school. Waning loyalty is a signal for change.

Honesty

The Bible says that our yes is to mean yes, and our no is to mean no. Absolute honesty is needed in all of your relationships within the school. Be a person of your word, a person of integrity. Let your spoken words and your written words be accurate, meaning what they say.

It is a simple matter to shade things a little bit in your favor through your choice of words. Recognize that temptation and avoid it. It is devastating to a school when teachers and administrators do not feel that they can trust each others' words. That is unsettling and shakes the very roots and fabric of the school.

Having an open spirit which is willing to admit you are wrong is a key to honesty. It is not a problem to be truthful when you have done well, but telling the truth when you have not done well is another problem, and is where the bite comes. No principal expects you to be perfect, and you should not expect that of him. You do not have to live behind a facade. Be honest before God and man and do not allow yourself to be bound by dishonesty.

Daily Attendance

Keep yourself in good condition so that you are ready to go each morning, including Mondays and Fridays, the days most frequently missed by school teachers. Some teachers drive themselves into the ground with a personal schedule that is too heavy. You want a balanced life and need spiritual, social, and physical activities to supplement the planning and grading that you do at home. Govern your activities rather than letting them control you. It is not right to miss school because fatigue or sickness have been brought on through your own mismanagement. Watch your diet, exercise, and rest.

Let the principal know as early as possible when you are going to be absent because of illness. It is not an easy thing to get substitutes and lead time is beneficial. It is better to let him know the night before. It not, call him as early as possible in the morning. It is unethical to call him about half an hour before school starts. You should be reprimanded if you do that.

Some teachers are so strong-willed that they do not want to admit that they are sick, and come to school when they should be home in bed. This is in contrast to the teacher who stays home with every sniffle or pain. It is not fair to your students or to yourself to come to school when you are sick. Stay at home. The school can afford the substitute.

Do not be slow in seeing the doctor when you are sick. An early start with medication may reduce the number of days you must miss. It is good to see the doctor the first day of your absence unless you are quite sure that you will be on your feet the next day. Above all, look to God for His hand of healing upon you.

Home Conditions

A teacher's home living conditions have a powerful effect upon him, and thus upon his teaching. Your home should be a place where you can relax and be renewed in your spirit and in your body. It should be free of tension, for teachers need the daily healing that a peaceful home brings.

Married teachers must guard their relationship to their spouse and children. Serious internal family problems will influence that teacher's performance in school far more than the teacher thinks. In addition, a man's prayers are hindered if he is not in right fellowship with his wife, according to the Bible. The same is true of the wife.

Single teachers who share homes or apartments sometimes find themselves in a poor combination. A change is in order as soon as possible. A few single teachers are better off living alone.

Appearance and Grooming

Students like teachers who look nice. They appreciate teachers whose clothing is fashionable rather than looking as if it came out of the missionary barrel. They like teachers whose hair is styled well. It is not only the students who will appreciate these things about you. Everyone does.

This does not mean that you have to look as if you stepped out of the pages of the latest fashion magazine. It means that you should pay attention to yourself and care about your appearance. True, your fellowship with God is primary, but do not neglect the outward man which everyone sees.

Spend enough money in your budget for clothes and grooming to look nice. It will lift your morale too. Keep your eyes open for sales and ask God to give you good buys to stretch your money. He is able to provide for you in this area as you trust Him.

Being Approachable

A teacher has a place of honor and respect because of his ministry. This position should not make you unapproachable as a person. Be personable and open, unthreatened, with everyone. Do not be overly defensive and never be intimidating.

Most students pick up their parents' attitudes toward teachers. Sometimes parents were afraid of their teachers and transmit a fear to their children about teachers that is beyond proper respect. Be sensitive to this and break it down quietly. You want respect, but not fear. Love casts out fear.

People will hesitate to approach you if they feel that you

are always judgmental. If they feel uneasy around you because you project the image of constantly judging them, they will avoid you. This does not mean that you condone sin. It means that you follow the example of Jesus who was free in his spirit to talk to even vile sinners, and they felt free to talk to Him, a remarkable combination.

Sense of Humor

Even a Christian school can get grim at times without some fun. A sense of humor is helpful to yourself and to others. Be able to laugh at hourself. A good laugh can do wonders for your class and for you.

Be careful not to ridicule your students or colleagues with your humor. If it is not fun for them too, do not say it or do it. Do not carry things too far, for it is a school and not a camp. If your humor backfires, and it sometimes does, go to the people involved and straighten it out with them. If you showed poor judgment in the humor, apologize and assure them that you have learned your lesson.

Personal Finance

Christian school personnel are not overpaid and must watch their money carefully or they find that too much of the month is left before next payday. It is easy to borrow money, but it is very hard to pay it back. It is also expensive.

Be realistic and live within your means. Accept your financial status as from God and do not be jealous of other teachers who have inherited money and do not have to live on their school salary. Do not envy other Christians whose living standards are higher because they make more money. Do not try to keep up with them by borrowing money.

Jesus said that a man's life does not consist of the abundance of the things which he possesses. He also said that if we seek first the kingdom of God and His righteousness, all these things shall be added unto us. Serving Him in the school and seeing Him provide for us and for our families is an evidence of His faithfulness which is great, and of His mercies which are new every morning.

Your attitude toward money is one of the strongest influences upon your Christian life. Jesus said that it is impossible to serve money and to serve God.

Family Priority

The order of priorities for the teacher is God, family, and school. There is no profit for a married teacher to serve the children of others and lose his own son or daughter. Life permits no rerun and this loss cannot be regained.

Sometimes a Christian school teacher is too loyal to the school to the detriment of his own family. It is as if he were married to the school, not to his wife. It is as if the students were his own, to the neglect of his own. This is not right.

God will give you time in your busy life to do right by your family, if you will use the time that way. You may not have the quantity of time that others have, but you will have quality. One of the greatest proofs of your Christian school ministry will be the fact that your own children have grown up and are walking with God. This gives credibility to your counsel with parents as they seek to raise their children to walk with God.

Moonlighting

Christian school teaching is demanding. It is hard to do it well and hold another part-time job. Try to live within your salary, budgeting carefully, so that you will not need additional work. If that is impossible, it would be good to talk to your principal to explain to him what you are planning. You will be on your own time, but this is bound to influence your classroom performance and he should know about it. Try not to moonlight any longer than is absolutely necessary. Pray hard about the matter.

The salary scales in some Christian schools are so low and unrealistic that God may be showing you through moonlighting that you should seek employment at another Christian school that follows the scriptural principle that the laborer is worthy of his hire. This would not be a move for unspiritual reasons because the Bible says that the Christian who does not take care of his own family is an infidel and has denied the faith.

Teaching in another Christian school with a reasonable wage would allow you to spend those moonlighting hours on your teaching and would be beneficial to you, to your family, and to your students. Project your present situation for the next five years and see if you like what you see. If you do not, ask God to transfer you next year and get your applications out right now. Many teachers are looking for jobs in Christian schools.

Patience

Miss Norma LaShure, one of the first grade teachers at D.C., said that her children had asked her the following four questions by 10 A.M. on the very first day of school: (1) When do we go home? (2) When do we eat lunch? (3) Do we have to take naps? (4) Are you going to teach us how to read today? That is an enjoyable list, but it underscores the need for patience on the part of the teacher. It might take her more than one day to teach them how to read.

Most of our ministry follows what the Bible calls line upon line and precept upon precept, here a little and there a little. We have to keep at it, faithfully. Looking back over a longer period of time we can see progress and some days we see spurts, but usually things do not happen too fast and it is hard to measure what was accomplished in one day. God encourages us in our patience for it is His way. He promises that harvest will come.

Close of the Year

Everyone is in a hurry to get going at the end of the school year. Teachers are as eager as students to get away from school, even though they love it, and get into summer plans of work and vacation. This is expected and natural for it is a long hard year. Principals also enjoy summer.

Most schools have a checkout list for teachers telling them everything to be done prior to leaving for the summer. Do not allow your impatience to leave distort your sense of responsibility to complete things. Give yourself enough time to do everything without feeling that you are under the gun because you have made your personal schedule too tight and must get moving. Finish well. Then, have a good summer. You earned it.

Try to spend a little extra time with the Lord.

Chapter Six

PAYING
THE PRICE

Christian school teaching is an effective ministry, a good work. It is a worthwhile expenditure of energy, in fact, of life. The teacher fulfills his presenting of himself to God in terms of Romans 12:1, 2, through his daily work in the classroom.

Make no mistake, let it be clear: There is a price to be paid. If a teacher is going to give his life to this work, the price will not only reach him, it will reach his wife and his children. There will be numerous times when the pressures to leave the Christian school ministry are intense. But we have put our hand to this plow and we must not turn back.

Although there is a price, God is with us. When we do His will our wives and our children will not suffer. Our Father is not like that. In fact, our children are encouraged to serve God themselves, for they are experiencing the provision of God for them as they are growing up in a Christian school teacher's home. We need to encourage our children as David did his son Solomon when he said, "And thou, Solomon, my son, know thou the God of thy father, and serve him with a perfect heart and with a willing mind: for the Lord searcheth all hearts, and understandeth all the imaginations of the thoughts: if thou seek him, he will be found of thee; but if thou forsake him, he will cast thee off forever." 1 Chronicles 28:9.

David also stands as an example to us of a man who was willing to pay the price in order to do God's will. A clear example of his attitude is given in 2 Samuel 24. He had sinned against the Lord by numbering the valiant men that drew the sword in both Israel and Judah. God judged him by killing 70,000 men from Dan even to Beer-sheba. This shattered David and he spoke to the angel of the Lord who smote the men and asked that his hand be upon David and upon his father's house, for he was the sinner in the matter since God had clearly said not to number the men.

The same day the prophet, Gad, came to David with a message from the Lord. He instructed David to go up and rear an altar unto the Lord in the threshingfloor of Araunah the Jebusite. Araunah saw the king and his entourage coming. He went out, bowed on his face upon the ground, and asked David what he wanted. David replied that he wanted to buy Araunah's threshingfloor and build an altar to the Lord so that the plague against the people would stop. Araunah responded by saying that he would give David whatever he wanted, including oxen for burnt sacrifice and threshing instruments and other instruments for wood. The Bible says that all these things did Araunah, as a king, give unto the king, saying, "The Lord thy God accept thee."

At this point the attitude of David, who was the man after God's own heart and the sweet psalmist of Israel, comes through as an example to us. He responded to the gracious offer of Araunah by saying, "Nay, but I will surely buy it of thee at a price: neither will I offer burnt-offerings unto the Lord my God of that which doth cost me nothing." David bought the threshingfloor and the oxen for fifty shekels of silver. He paid the price. He built the altar unto the Lord, offered burnt offerings and peace offerings, and the Lord was intreated for the land. The plague was stayed from Israel.

This same incident is recorded in 1 Chronicles 21. This passage brings out the fact that David also bought the whole piece of ground on which the threshingfloor was built for six hundred shekels of gold, in addition to the fifty shekels of silver for the floor and for the oxen recorded in 2 Samuel 24.

The account in Chronicles is more complete. This is particularly significant when examining David's response to Araunah when he wanted to give everything to David. Not only did David say that he would buy everything, twice in the Chronicles text it is recorded that David said he would pay the full price, not just a price, the full price. For example, David said in 1 Chronicles 21:24, "Nay; but I will verily buy it for the full price: for I will not take that which is thine for the Lord, nor offer burnt-offerings without cost."

David paid the price. David paid the full price. David would not accept the gift of something belonging to another person to give that to God. David wanted it to cost him personally when he gave something to the Lord.

The sequel to this incident is beautiful. King David died and Solomon his son reigned in his stead. Prior to his death, David charged Solomon to build the temple of the Lord. Solomon took that to heart and began to build the temple. Here is the wondrous sequel: Solomon built the temple on the very ground which David had bought from Araunah in the incident just discussed. The Scriptures say in 2 Chronicles 3:1, "Then Solomon began to build the house of the Lord at Jerusalem in mount Moriah, where the Lord appeared unto David his father, in the place that David had prepared in the threshingfloor of Araunah the Jebusite."

In the place where a father was willing to pay the full price for an offering to God, years later his son built a temple to God. God continues to do that today. In a Christian school where a teacher is willing to pay the full price, pouring out his very life a day at a time, God builds temples in the lives of his students.

This does not happen without paying the price in full.

"Lord, help me to pay the full
price for Jesus' sake. Amen."

Chapter Seven

A SELECTED BIBLIOGRAPHY
OF HELPFUL BOOKS

The listing of a book in this bibliography is not necessarily an endorsement by the author or the publisher.

Adams, Jay E. **Competent to Counsel.** Nutley, New Jersey: Presbyterian and Reformed, 1972.

Alexander, John. **Managing Our Work.** Downers Grove, Illinois: Inter Varsity Press, 1972.

Anderson, John B. **Vision and Betrayal in America.** Waco, Texas: Word Books, 1975.

Armerding, Hudson. **Christianity and the World of Thought.** Chicago, Illinois: Moody Press, 1968.

Baldwin, A. Graham and Gaebelein, Frank E. and Harrison, Carl G. Jr. **Commitment and the School Community.** Greenwich, Connecticut: Leabury Press, 1960.

Barclay, William. **Educational Ideals in the Ancient World.** Grand Rapids: Baker Book House, 1974.

Barker, Charles A. **American Convictions.** Philadelphia: J.B. Lippincott Co., 1970.

Barnes, Harry Elmer. **An Intellectual and Cultural History of the Western World.** Rev. ed., Vol 3, New York: Dover Publications, 1965.

Bellah, Robert N. **The Broken Covenant.** New York: The Seabury Press,, 1975.

Benson, Clarence H. **A Popular History of Christian Education.** Chicago: Moody Press, 1943.

Bereday, George Z.F. and Lauwerys, Joseph A., eds. **The World Year Book of Education, 1966: Church and State in Education.** New York: Harcourt, Brace & World, 1966.

Beversluis, Nicholas Henry. **Christian Philosophy of Education.** Grand Rapids: National Union of Christian Schools, 1971.

Bigg, Charles. **The Church Task Under the Roman Empire.** Oxford: Clarendon Press, 1905.

Billings, Robert J. **A Guide to the Christian School.** Hammond, Indiana: Hyles-Anderson, 1970.

Blamires, Harry. **The Christian Mind.** London: William Clowes and Sons, 1966.

Blanshard, Paul. **Religion and the Schools: The Great Controversy.** Boston: Beacon Press, 1963.

Blinderman, Abraham. **Three Early Champions of Education: Benjamin Franklin, Benjamin Rush, and Noah Webster.** Bloomington, Indiana: The Phi Delta Kappa Educational Foundations, 1976.

Boles, Donald B. **The Two Swords.** Ames: Iowa State University Press, 1967.

Bolton, Barbara J. **Children, Grades 1-6. . . Ways to Help Them Learn.** Glendale, California: Gospel Light Publishers, 1972.

Bowen, James. **A History of Western Education.** New York: St. Martin's Press, 1975.

Brinton, Crane. **The Shaping of Modern Thought.** Englewood Cliffs: Prentice-Hall, 1964.

Brinton, Howard H. **Quaker Education in Theory and Practice.** Pendle Hill Pamphlet, 1940.

Bronowski, J. and Bruce Mazlish. **The Western Intellectual Traditions: From Leonardo to Hegel.** New York: Harper and Row, 1960.

Brown, B. Franks. **Education by Appointment: New Approach to Independent Study.** West Nyack, New York: Parker Publishing, 1968.

Bruner, Jerome S. **The Process of Education.** Cambridge, Massachusetts: Harvard University Press, 1960.

Butts, R. Freeman. **The American Tradition in Religion and Education.** Boston: The Beacon Press, 1951.

Byrne, Herbert W. **A Christian Approach to Education.** Grand Rapids: Zondervan Publishing Company, 1961.

Cailliet, Emile. **The Christian Approach to Culture.** New York, New York: Abingdon-Cokesbury Press.

Carlson, Violet. **The Christian Educator's File.** Chicago, Illinois: Moody Press, 1954.

Childs, John L. **Education and Morals.** New York: Appleton-Century-Crofts Inc., 1950.

Christensen, Larry. **The Christian Family.** Minneapolis, Minnesota: Bethany Fellowship Company, 1970.

Clark, Burton R. **The Problems of American Education.** New York: New York Times Book, 1975.

Clark, Gordon H. **A Christian Philosophy of Education.** Grand Rapids: Wm. B. Eerdmans, 1946.

Cole, Luella W. **A History of Education, Socrates To Montessori.** New York: Holt, Rinehart and Winston, 1962.

Compayr'e, Gabriel. **The History of Pedagogy.** Translated by W.H. Payne. Boston: D.C. Heath & Company, 1897.

Conant. **The American High School Today.** New York, New York: McGraw-Hill Book Company, 1959.

Cox, Harvey. **The Secular City,** rev. ed. New York: Macmillan, 1966.

Crabb, Lawrence, J. **Basic Principles of Biblical Counseling.** Grand Rapids, Michigan: Zondervan Press, 1975.

Crain, Robert L. **The Politics of School Desegregation.** Garden City, New York: Doubleday, 1969.

Cronbach, Lee J. **Educational Psychology.** New York, New York: Harcourt, Brace & World, 1954.

Culver, Robert Duncan. **Toward a Biblical View of Civil Government.** Chicago: Moody Press, 1974.

Davidheiser, Bolton. **Evolution and Christian Faith.** Nutley, New Jersey: Presbyterian and Reformed Publishing Co., 1969.

DeJong, Norman. **Education in the Truth.** Nutley, New Jersey: Presbyterian and Reformed Publishing Co., 1969.

Dewey, John. **Democracy and Education, An Introduction to the Philosophy of Education.** New York: The Macmillan Company, 1923.

_____ . **Ethical Principles Underlying Education.** Chicago: University of Chicago Press, 1903.

Dillenberger, John and Claude Welch. **Protestant Christianity.** New York: Charles Scribner's Sons, 1954.

Dismanson, H., Hong, H. and Quanbeck, W. **Christian Faith and the Liberal Arts.** Minneapolis, Minnesota: Augsburg Publishing House, 1960.

Dobson, James. **Dare to Discipline.** Wheaton, Illinois: Tyndale House Publishers, 1972.

_____ . **Hide or Seek.** Old Tappan, New Jersey: Fleming H. Revell Company, 1974.

Dolbeare, Kenneth M., and Patricia Dolbeare. **American Idealogies.** Chicago: Markham Publishing Company, 1971.

Dooyeweerd, Herman. **A New Critique of Theoretical Thought.** 4 vols. Translated by David H. Freeman, et al. Philadelphia: Presbyterian and Reformed Publishing Co., 1953.

Douglas, William O. **The Bible and the Schools.** Boston: Little, Brown & Company, 1966.

Drake, Gordon V. **Is the School House the Proper Place to Teach Raw Sex?** Tulsa, Oklahoma: Christian Crusade Publications, 1968.

Drazin, Nathan. **History of Jewish Education From 515 B.C.E. to 220 C.E.** Baltimore: The John Hopkins Press, 1940.

Dunlop, Richard S. **Professional Problems in School Counseling Practice.** International Textbook Company, 1968.

Dupois, Adrian M. **Philosophy of Education in Historical Perspective.** Chicago: Rand McNally and Co., 1966.

Eavey, C.B. **History of Christian Education.** Chicago, Illinois: Moody Press, 1964.

_____. **Principles of Teaching For Christian Teachers.** Grand Rapids, Michigan: Zondervan Press, n.d.

Edwards, Lawrence O. **Creative Bible Teaching.** Chicago, Illinois: Moody Press, 1970.

Ehler, Sidney Z. and Morrall, John B., eds. **Church and State Through the Centuries.** New York: Biblo and Tannen, 1967.

Ehrensaft, Philip and Amitai Etzioni, eds. **Anatomies of America.** London: The Macmillan Company, 1969.

Fakkema, Mark A. **Christian Philosophy.** Chicago: Christian Schools Service, Inc., n.d.

_____. **Christian Philosophy and its Educational Implications.** 4 vols. Chicago: National Association of Christian Schools, n.d.

Fellman, David. **The Supreme Court and Education.** New York: Teachers College, 1969.

Fichter, Joseph H. **Parochial School: A Sociological Study.** Garden City, New York: Doubleday & Company, Inc., 1964.

French, Willa and Associates. **Behavioral Goals of General Education in High School.** New York, New York: Russell Sage Foundation, 1957.

Fuller, Edmund. **The Christian Idea of Education.** New Haven, Connecticut: Yale University Press, 1962.

Gabriel, Ralph Henry. **The Course of American Democratic Thought.** New York: Ronald Press Co., 1956.

Gaebelein, Frank E. **A Varied Harvest.** Grand Rapids, Michigan: William B. Eerdmans Publishing Company, 1967.

_____. **Christian Education in a Democracy.** New York, New York: Oxford University Press, 1954.

_____. **The Pattern of God's Truth.** New York, New York: Oxford University Press, 1954.

_____, and Harrison Earl G. Jr. and Swing, William L. **Education For Decision.** New York, New York: Leabury Press, 1963.

Gangel, Kenneth O. **Competent to Lead.** Chicago, Illinois: Moody Press, 1974.

_____. **Twenty-four Ways to Improve Your Teaching.** Wheaton, Illinois: Victor Publications, n.d.

Garrick, Gene. **Making the Christian School Christian.** Sepulveda, California: The Development of Baptist Day Schools, 1974.

Getz, Gene A. **Sharpening the Focus of the Church.** Chicago: Moody Press, 1974.

Glasser, William. **Schools Without Failure.** New York: Harper and Row, 1969.

_____. **The Identity Society.** New York: Harper and Row, 1972.

Glogaw, Krause, Wexler. **Developing a Successful Elementary Media Center.** Nyack, New York: Parker Publishing, 1972.

Goslin, David A. **The School in Contemporary Society.** Chicago: Scott, Foresman, 1965.

Gothard, Bill. **Basic Youth Conflicts, Advanced Leadership Guide.** Available only through seminar attendance.

Gregory, John Milton. **The Seven Laws of Teaching.** Grand Rapids, Michigan: Baker Book House, 1975.

Grob, Gerald N. and Robert N. Beck, eds. **Ideas in America.** New York: The Free Press, 1970.

Grueningen, John Paul. **Toward a Christian Philosophy of Higher Education.** Philadelphia, Pennsylvania: Westminster Press, 1957.

Guder, Eileen. **To Live in Love.** Grand Rapids, Michigan: Zondervan Press, 1967.

Guinness, Os. **The Dust of Death.** Downers Grove: Inter-Varsity, 1975.

Hakes, Edward, ed. **An Introduction to Evangelical Christian Education.** Chicago: Moody Press, 1964.

Handy, Robert T. **A Christian America: Protestant Hopes and Historical Realities.** New York: Oxford University Press, 1971.

Harris, R. Laird. **Inspiration and Canonicity of the Bible.** Grand Rapids: Zondervan Publishing House, 1969.

Hefley, James C. **Textbooks on Trial.** Wheaton, Illinois: Victor Books, 1976.

Hamphill, Martha Locke. **Weekday Ministry With Young Children.** Valley Forge, Pennsylvania: Judson Press, 1973.

Hertzler, Daniel. **Mennonite Education: Why and How?** Scottdale, Pennsylvania: Herald Press, 1971.

Hunt. **Honey for a Child's Heart.** Grand Rapids, Michigan: Zondervan Press, 1969.

Jahsman, Allen Hart. **What's Lutheran in Education?** St. Louis: Concordia Publishing House, 1960.

Jeffries, Derwin J. **Your Child Is Crying.** Titusville, New Jersey: The Home and School Press, 1970.

Jencks, Christopher and David Riesman. **The Academic Revolution.** Garden City, New York: Doubleday, 1969.

Johnson, James A. **Foundations of American Education.** Boston: Allyn and Bacon, Inc., 1972.

Jones, Charles. **Life is Tremendous.** Wheaton, Illinois: Tyndale House, n.d.

Kane, William T. **History of Education.** Chicago: Loyola University Press, 1954.

Karlin, Jules, **Man's Behavior.** New York: The Macmillan Company, 1967.

Kennedy, David M. and Paul A. Robinson. **Social Thought in America and Europe.** Boston: Little, Brown, and Co., 1970.

Kennedy, William B. **The Shaping of Protestant Education.** New York: Association Press, 1966.

Kent, Charles Foster. **The Great Teachers of Judaism and Christianity.** New York: Eaton & Mains, 1911.

Kienel, Paul A. **America Needs Bible Centered Families and Schools.** La Habra, California: P.K. Books, 1976.

——————. **The Christian School: Why It Is Right for Your Child.** Wheaton: Victor Books, 1976.

——————. **The Philosophy of Christian School Education.** Whittier, California: Western Association of Christian Schools, 1977.

Kik, Jacob Marcellus. **The Supreme Court and Prayer in the Public School.** Philadelphia: Presbyterian and Reformed Publishing Co., 1963.

Kneller, George F. **Introduction to the Philosophy of Education.** New York: John Wiley and Sons, Inc., 1954.

Koerner, James D. **Who Controls American Education?** Boston: Beacon Press, 1969.

Krause, Victor C. **Lutheran Elementary School in Action:** St. Louis: Concordia Publishing Company, 1963.

Kraushaar, Otto F. **American Nonpublic School.** Baltimore: The Johns Hopkins University Press, 1972.

——————. **Private Schools: From the Puritan to the Present.** Bloomington, Indiana: The Phi Delta Kappa Educational Foundation, 1976.

Kroll, Arthur M., ed. **Issues in American Education.** New York: Oxford University Press, 1970.

Krutch, Joseph 'Wood.' **Human Nature and the Human Condition.** New York: Random House, Inc., 1959.

La Haye, Timothy. **Spirit Controlled Temperament.** Wheaton, Illinois: Tyndale House, 1966.

114

Langford, Glenn. **Philosophy and Education: An Introduction.** New York, New York: Macmillan Company, 1971.

LeBar, Lois E. **Education That is Christian.** Old Tappan, New Jersey: Fleming H. Revell Co., 1958.

_____. **Focus on People in Church Education.** Old Tappan, Revell, 1968.

Leenhauts, Keith J. **A Father, A Son, and a Three Mile Run.** Grand Rapids, Michigan: Zondervan Press, 1975.

LeFevre, Perry. **The Christian Teacher.** New York, New York: Abingdon Press, 1958.

Lemlech, Johanna, and Marks, Merle B. **The American Teacher: 1776-1976.** Bloomington, Indiana: The Phi Delta Kappa Educational Foundation, 1976.

Lewis, C.S. **Mere Christianity.** New York, New York: MacMillan Company, 1968.

_____. **The Abolition of Man.** New York: The Macmillan Company, 1947.

Lieberman, Myron. **The Future of Public Education.** New York: Oxford University Press, 1962.

Lockerbie, D. Bruce. **The Way They Should Go.** New York: Oxford University Press, 1972.

Love, Robert. **How To Start Your Own School.** New York: The Macmillan Company, 1973.

Lutzer, Erwin W. **Failure, the Back Door to Success.** Chicago, Illinois: Moody Press, 1966.

Machen, J. Gresham. **Christianity and Liberalism.** Grand Rapids: Wm. B. Eerdmans, 1923.

Matson, Thomas B. **Christianity and World Issues.** New York: The Macmillan Company, 1957.

May, Philip. **Which Way to Educate?** Chicago: Moody Press, 1975.

Mayer, Frederick. **A History of Educational Thought.** Columbus, Ohio: Charles E. Merrill Books, 1960.

Mayers, Marvin K., Lawrence Richards, and Robert Webber. **Reshaping Evangelical Higher Education.** Grand Rapids: Zondervan Publishing House, 1972.

McGiffert, A.C. **Protestant Thought Before Kant.** New York: Harper and Row, 1961.

Mensing, Morella. **Today's Christian Kindergarten.** St. Louis, Missouri: Concordia Publishing House, 1972.

Millar, L. **Christian Education in the First Four Centuries.** London: The Faith Press Ltd., 1946.

Moffett, James. **A Student-Centered Language Arts Curriculum, Handbook for Teachers.** Boston, Massachusetts: Houghton-Mifflin, 1973.

Monroe, Paul. **A Textbook in the History of Education.** New York: The Macmillan Company, 1905.

Morris, Nathan. **The Jewish School.** New York: Jewish Education Committee Press, 1964.

Morris, Van Cleve. **Modern Movements in Educational Philosophy.** Boston: Houghton Mifflin Company, 1969.

Morris, Van Cleve and Pai, Young. **Philosophy and the American School.** Boston: Houghton Mifflin Co., 1976.

Murray, Alfred L. **Psychology For Christian Teachers.** Grand Rapids, Michigan: Zondervan Press, 1956.

Nazigian, Arthur. **Teach Them Diligently.** Brookhaven, Pennsylvania: The Christian Academy, 1974.

Nee, Watchman. **Spiritual Authority.** New York, New York: Christian Fellowship Publishing, 1972.

Newbury, Josephine. **Church Kindergarten Resource Book.** Richmond. Virginia: C.L.C. Press, 1964.

NUCS. **Course of Study for Christian Schools.** Grand Rapids, Michigan: William B. Eerdmans, 1963.

Nyquist, Ewald, Hawes, Gene R. **A Sourcebook for Parents and Teachers.** New York, New York: Bantam Books, 1972.

O'Neill, William F. **Selected Educational Heresies.** Glenview, Illinois: Scott, Foresman and Company, 1969.

Park, Joe. **Reading in the Philosophy of Education.** New York: The Macmillan Company, 1968.

Paul, Leslie. **Alternatives to Christian Belief: A Critical Survey of the Contemporary Search of Meaning.** New York: Doubleday, 1967.

Pentecost, Dwight J. **Design for Discipleship.** Grand Rapids, Michigan: Zondervan Press, 1971.

_____. **Design to be Like Him.** Chicago, Illinois: Moody Press, 1968.

Person, Peter P. **An Introduction to Christian Education.** Grand Rapids: Baker Book House, 1958.

Peterson, J.A. **Who Runs Your Life?** Lincoln, Nebraska: Back to the Bible, 1967.

Pines, Maya. **Revolution in Learning.** New York: Harper and Row, 1966.

Power, Edward W. **Evolution of Educational Doctrine.** New York: Appleton-Century-Crofts, 1969.

Price, J.M. Chapman et al. **A Survey of Religious Education.** New York: The Ronald Press, 1959.

Probe Ministries International. **Institute of Christian Apologetics.** Dallas, Texas: Probe Ministries International, 1973.

Rafferty, Max. **Max Rafferty on Education.** New York: Devin-Adair Company, 1968.

_____. **Our Schools and the Future.** New Rochelle, New York: America's Future, Inc., 1973.

_____. **Suffer, Little Children.** New York: Devin-Adair Company, 1962.

Ramm, Bernard, **Protestant Biblical Interpretation.** Grand Rapids: Baker Book House, 1970.

Randel, I.L. **The Cult of Uncertainty.** New York: Avno Press and The New York Times, 1971.

Revel, Jean-Francois. **Without Marx or Jesus.** Garden City, New York: Doubleday & Company, 1970.

Rice, John R. **Our God-Breathed Book — The Bible.** Murfreesboro, Tennessee: Sword of the Lord Publishers, 1969.

Richards, Lawrence O. **A Theology of Christian Education.** Grand Rapids: Zondervan Publishing House, 1975.

_____. **Youth Ministry.** Grand Rapids, Michigan: Zondervan Press, 1965.

Runner, H. Evan. **The Relation of the Bible to Learning.** Ontario, Canada: Wedge Publishing Foundation, 1970.

Rushdoony, Rousas J. **Intellectual Schizophrenia.** Grand Rapids: Baker Book House, 1961.

_____. **The Messianic Character of American Education.** Philadelphia: Presbyterian and Reformed Publishing Co., 1963.

Saller, Sylvester, J. **Second Revised Catalogue of the Ancient Synagogues of the Holy Land.** Jerusalem: Franciscan Printing Press, 1972.

Sanders, Oswald, J. **Spiritual Clinic.** Chicago, Illinois: Moody Press, 1958.

_____. **Spiritual Leadership.** Chicago, Illinois: Moody Press, 1958.

Sanderson, John W. Jr. **Encounter in the Non Christian Era.** Grand Rapids: Zondervan, 1970.

Schaeffer, Francis A. **Back to Freedom and Dignity.** Downers Grove, Illinois: Inter-Varsity Press, 1972.

_____. **The Church at the End of the 20th Century.** Downers Grove, Illinois: Inter-Varsity Press, 1970.

_____. **Death in the City.** Downers Grove, Illinois: Inter-Varsity Press, 1969.

_____. **Escape from Reason.** London: Inter-Varsity Press, 1968.

_____. **The God Who is There.** Downers Grove, Illinois: Inter-Varsity Press, 1968.

_____. **How Should We Then Live?** Old Tappan, New Jersey: Fleming H. Revell Company, 1976.

_____ . **True Spirituality.** Wheaton, Illinois: Tyndale House, 1971.

Schneider, Kenneth R. **Destiny of Change.** New York: Holt, Rinehart, and Winston, Inc., 1968.

Schuller, Robert. **Move Ahead With Possibility Thinking.** New York, New York: Pyramid Publications, 1967.

Sherrill, Lewis J. **The Rise of Christian Education.** New York: The Macmillan Company, 1944.

Silberman, Charles E. **Crisis in the Classroom.** New York: Random House, 1970.

Small, Walter H. **Early New England Schools.** New York, New York: Arno Press and the New York Times, 1969.

Smith, James A. **Adventures in Communication.** Boston, Massachusetts: Allyn & Bacon, 1972.

Smith, Philip G. **Philosophy of Education.** New York: Harper and Row, 1965.

Smith, Robert W. ed. **Christ and the Modern Mind.** Downers Grove, Illinois: Inter-Varsity Press, 1972.

Soderholm, Marjorie. **Understanding the Pupil.** Grand Rapids, Michigan: Baker Book House, 1956.

Spier, J.M. **An Introduction to Christian Philosophy.** Translated by David H. Freeman. Nutley, New Jersey: Craig Press, 1966.

Steensma, Geraldine J. **To Those Who Teach: Keys For Decision Making.** Signal Mountain, Tennessee: Signal, 1971.

Stinnette, Charles R. Sr. **Learning in Theological Perspective.** New York, New York: Association Press, 1965.

Sukenik, E.L. **Ancient Synagogues in Palestine and Greece.** London: Oxford University Press, 1934.

Swift, Fletcher H. **Education in Ancient Israel to 70 A.D.** Chicago: The Open Court Publishing Company, 1919.

Thatcher, David A. **Teaching, Loving and Self-Directed Learning.** Pacific Palisades, California: Goodyear Publishing Company, 1973.

Towns, Elmer L. **Have the Public Schools "Had It?".** Thomas Nelson Inc., n.d.

_____. **A History of Religious Educators.** Grand Rapids: Baker Book House, 1975.

Tozer, A.W. **The Pursuit of God.** Harrisburg, Pennsylvania: Christian Publications, Inc., 1958.

Tussman, Joseph, ed. **The Supreme Court on Church and State.** New York: Oxford University Press, 1962.

Tyack, David B. **Turning Points in American Educational History.** Waltham, Massachusetts: Blaisdell Publishing Company, 1967.

Ulrich, Robert. **Education in Western Culture.** New York: Harcourt, Brace and World, Inc., 1961.

_____. **A History of Religious Education.** New York, New York: New York University Press, 1968.

Van Til, Cornelius. **The Dilemma of Education.** Grand Rapids, Michigan; NUCS., 1954.

_____. **Essays on Christian Education.** Presbyterian and Reformed Publishing Company, 1974.

Wiersbe, Warren W. **Be Joyful.** Downers Grove, Illinois: Scripture Press, 1974.

Wilds, Elmer H. **The Foundations of Modern Education.** New York: Holt, Rinehart and Winston, Inc., 1961.

Wilson, Clifford, **Jesus the Teacher.** Mt. Waverly, Australia: Word of Truth Publications, 1974.

Worrell, Edward K. **Restoring God to Education.** Wheaton: Van Kampen Press, 1950.

Woodbridge, Doreen. **Take This Child.** Greenville, South Carolina: Bob Jones University Press, 1972.

Zuck, Roy B. **The Holy Spirit in Your Teaching.** Wheaton, Illinois: Scripture Press, 1963.

Zuck, Roy B. and Clark, Robert. **Childhood Education and the Church.** Chicago, Illinois: Moody Press, 1975.